THE WORLD OF AGATHA CHRISTIE

Reprinted in 2010 by SevenOaks
An imprint of the Carlton Publishing Group
20 Mortimer Street
London W1T 3JW

1 3 5 7 9 10 8 6 4 2

A CIP catalogue record for this book is available from the British Library

ISBN 978 1 86200 768 0

Printed and bound in Dubai

THE WORLD OF AGATHA CHRISTIE

THE FACTS AND FICTION BEHIND THE WORLD'S GREATEST CRIME WRITER

MARTIN FIDO

SEVENOAKS

Contents

Agatha Christie
Three Blind Mice
PERSIAN MINIATURE PAINTING
A SURVEY OF PERSIAN ART
ARTHUR U. POPE
OXFORD
A SURVEY OF PERSIAN ART
OXFORD
A SURVEY OF PERSIAN ART
OXFORD

Introduction

Agatha Christie was like one of her own protagonists. A woman whose outer colouring camouflaged her inner character. Her colouring was that of the conventional upper-middle class wife leading a formal, dull and dutiful life, who just happened to write an enormous number of detective stories. Exciting personalities bursting with brains abounded among the middlebrow detective writers of the interwar Golden Age: Oxford-educated Anglo-Catholic Dorothy Sayers, who translated Dante and the *Chanson de Roland*: Mgr Reginald Knox, a sparkling intellectual wit. Margery Allingham, whose annual parties brought together bright lights from the world of arts, literature and fashion; "Michael Innes", in private life the Christ Church don, J.I.M. Stuart.

In private life Agatha Christie was, first a golf-playing stockbroker's wife, then Lady Mallowan, the tongue-tied wife of an academic archaelogist whose great excavation at Nimrud never caught the popular imagination in the way that Tutankhamen's tomb or the Palace at Knossos did. Other detective writers produced their whodunnits as side activities in a busy life: a poet who would become laureate (Cecil Day Lewis as Nicholas Blake), or a vital force in New Zealand theatre who would be honoured for such work (Ngaio Marsh). Dame Agatha, honoured wholly and solely for her whodunnits and thrillers, apparently reached her zenith at the typewriter, and was capable of nothing more.

What a startling camouflage! Poirot might assemble all the above writers for his great final exposé and address them thus:

"So, Mgr Knox, you have translated the Bible from Latin? Can you read even the simplest cuneiform? The language of Ancient Assyria? *Voilà*, Mrs Christie had her own apartment in a Mesopotamian excavation labelled "Beit Agatha" – House of Agatha – in cuneiform inscription.

"Miss Sayers, you give us much of the dashing Lord Peter Wimsey and his so fast driving and his so romantic attachment to Miss Harriet Vane. But your, life, I think, it was not so romantic, *hein*? It was the young Mrs Christie who truly enjoyed the fast cars, the romantic thrills, the love at first sight. It is this lady who was really the risk taking heroine of adventure.

"Which too I must stress to Miss Allingham, asking her what do they know of England who only England know? Indeed, apart from Mrs Christie who is there in this room who has travelled by mule over the desert, slept under a stalled car in the wilderness, flown in the little wire and canvas aeroplanes, travelled to Baghdad and Stamboul by such pioneering means that an occasional journey on the Orient Express was indeed a signal luxury!"

"Dame Ngaio, you question Dame Agatha's role in the world of the executant arts? But this is a woman who could have become a concert singer; would have attempted an operatic career had her voice been strong enough; played the piano to a high standard all her life; and as for theatre – had three plays at one time playing in the West End and still has the world's longest-running play in performance.

"Mr Stewart, you refer to scholarship. Dame Agatha knew more about middle eastern prehistoric pots than any other woman in the world. What is your area of similarly unique expertise? Mr Day Lewis, you question her general literary taste? She wrote verse appropriate to her age and station all her life. Her books are filled with quotations from poets ancient and modern – including T.S. Eliot.

"No, ladies and gentlemen. It is not the dull and retiring and boring product of finishing schools and bourgeois marriages whom Hercule Poirot perceives. It is the gifted and highly intelligent writer who was also a trained musician and photographer, a self-taught archaeologist; a woman who earned her own living and bought her own houses. I salute the true, the prime heroine of the fictional puzzles for the little grey cells, Dame Agatha Christie."

Time Chart

1878 Fred Miller marries Clar(iss)a Boehmer

1879 Margaret Frary (Madge) Miller born

1880 Louis Montant (Monty) Miller born
Clara buys Ashfield

1890 Agatha Mary Clarissa Miller born

1895–6 Miller family living in France

1901 Monty joins East Surrey Regiment
Fred Miller dies

1902 Madge marries James Watts
AC meets Nan Watts

1906 AC to Paris finishing and music schools

1910–11 AC makes debut in Cairo

1912 AC meets Archie Christie

1914 AC joins VAD
AC marries Archie

1916 *The Mysterious Affair at Styles* written

1919 Rosalind Margaret Clarissa Christie born

1920 *The Mysterious Affair at Styles* published by John Lane

1921 AC and Archie tour the world with Major Belcher

1924 Styles at Sunningdale purchased.
Charlotte ("Carlo") Fisher employed.

1926 *The Murder of Roger Ackroyd*
Clara Miller dies
Archie falls in love with Nancy Neele
AC disappears for 11 days

1927 AC divorces Archie

1928 AC visits Ur excavations

1929 AC meets Max Mallowan

1930 AC marries Max
Black Coffee produced

1934 AC Buys 48 Sheffield Terrace, W8 and Winterbrook House, Wallingford

1938 Sells Ashfield
Buys Greenway, near Dartmouth

1941 Max posted to Cairo
Rosalind marries Hubert Prichard
Agatha works in University College Hospital dispensary

1942 Mathew Prichard born

1944 Hubert killed in action

1948 Excavation at Nimrud begins

1949 Rosalind marries Anthony Hicks

1950 Madge dies

1952 *The Mousetrap* opens

1956 AC awarded CBE

1958 Nancy Neele Christie dies

1960 Max awarded CBE
Nimrud excavations completed
Mallowans go to Oberammergau

1962 Max elected Fellow of All Souls
Mathew captains Eton cricket team
Archie Christie dies

1967 Max awarded KBE

1971 AC awarded DBE

1973 *Postern of Fate* AC's last book

1976 AC dies at Winterbrook House
Buried at Cholsey

Family Tree

(1) Martha Messervey = Nathaniel Miller = (2) Margaret West "Auntie-Grannie"
(d.1888) (1827–1919)

Capt Frederick Boehmer = Mary Ann West "Grannie B"
(1816–1863) (1836–c.1913)

Frederick Ernest Henry

Frederick Alvah Miller = Clarissa (Clara) Boehmer
(1846–1901) (1854–1926)

Margaret Frary (Madge) = James Watts
(1878–1950)

Louis Montant (Monty)
(1880–c.1930)

(1) Archie Christie = **Agatha Mary Clarissa** = (2) Max Mallowan
(1890–1976) (1904–1978)

(1) Hubert Prichard = Rosalind Margaret Clarissa = (2) Anthony Hicks
(d.1944)

Mathew Caradoc Thomas
(b.1941)

The Lady

Agatha Christie, the quintessence of genteel English country life, was born Agatha Miller, half American – and definitely upper-class American at that. Her father, Frederick Alva Miller, traced his descent from an old New England family. Her grandfather, Nathaniel Miller, made his way to the top of the great New York firm of HB Chaflin where he set up a series of trusts that allowed his family to enjoy a life of leisure. Fred Miller was on the New York social register. As a young man he flirted with the heiress Jenny Jerome – who would later wed the Duke of Marlborough's younger son and become the mother of Winston Churchill. Mrs Pierpoint Morgan was a connection by marriage – the First Four Hundred of New York didn't come any more first than that.

When Fred Miller married his step-cousin Clara Boehmer and decided to leave New York society for England, he settled on Torquay as a home. This was the English Riviera, a regular holiday destination for the rich and leisured. There were palm trees on the promenade and winter gardens in the De Luxe Hotels. The Devonshire sun-trap was considered to be a perpetual playground for those who had little to do but play. Fred Miller devoted his life to mindless idleness. He strolled down to the club, read the papers, chatted with fellow members and remembered nothing of what he had read or said by the time he strolled back home.

He sent his eldest daughter Madge to Roedean and his son Monty to Harrow. Madge's "coming out" – the season when a debutante, a young upper-class girl, dressed her hair and went to a succession of dances to meet eligible young men – was held in New York.

Fred's second daughter, Agatha – evidently an accidental conception 10 years after the neat one-boy-one-girl family had been completed – was educated at home by nurses and governesses. Her life and writing would be coloured by the fact that she was born into an upper-class home and took for granted their habits and outlook.

But she did not envy the aristocracy. She enjoyed as merrily as anyone else the PG Wodehouse image of dotty old lords cultivating hobbies and eccentricities in ancestral stately homes, but she did not aspire to such grandeur herself. She confidently assumed an equality with their sons and daughters without a trace of social climbing. She was high enough up the ladder to feel no need to prove herself socially.

Not for her, when she became a writer, a detective hero such as Lord Peter Wimsey who fulfilled a clergyman's daughter's dream of the handsome, noble, talented brother of a duke. Not for her the improbable police inspectors who were really cadet members of noble families or notable poets in their own right. Agatha Miller was not impressed by such things. "The Lucy Girls" were friends of hers and she nearly married their brother Reggie. She would tell readers that they came from Warwickshire, that they had a bigger family home than her own, that they were some of the nicest people she knew. She didn't mention the fact that they were descended from that Sir Thomas Lucy whose prosecution of a local poacher sent young Will Shakespeare scampering off to London and fame. Unladylike boasting and self-consciousness were beneath her. To her admirers at the time, she seemed apolitical, classless and timelessly English. But in truth, she had a confidence that obscured class consciousness and endowed her with the simple certainty that whatever her kind thought was right.

The unstressed good manners and good form of Agatha Christie's work was never the calculated correctness of the genteel, however much Miss Marple's spinsterly severities might suggest it. Agatha Christie truly came of gentlefolk, She was, without having to think about it, a lady. It was this quality in her writing that charmed the generality of readers and tended to repel intellectual critics who resented the assumption that the author's unquestioned certainties were preferable to considered moral and social complexities.

The Family

Grandfather Nathaniel Frary Miller was the forebear Agatha most admired. Though the Millers were an old settler family going back to the seventeenth century, they fell on hard times in the 1820s, so Nathaniel had to work his way up from clerkship to partnership in one of New York's largest companies. All her life, Agatha would evince admiration for buccaneering self-made businessmen. In her fiction they would be forgiven for almost any offences except murder and treason. Twice she would contemplate using the name Nathaniel as a masculine *nom de plume.*

AGATHA AND HER FATHER AT ASHFIELD OUTSIDE THE "KAI KAI".

HB Chaflin's business brought one of the partners to England, where the Manchester merchants were a vital part of the world's fabric dealers. And working in one of the big hotels, frequented by the merchants, Nathaniel met Margaret West, one of 10 orphaned children brought up by elderly relatives and left with their own way to make in the world. Margaret was 36 when the elderly widower married her in 1863. They settled near Manchester and found to their regret that they were unable to have children of their own.

But Margaret had a younger sister in needy circumstances. Mary Ann "Polly" West married a dashing young captain of the Argyll Highlanders when she was only 16. Eleven years later he died, leaving her with three sons and a daughter to bring up on a miserable widow's pension. Nathaniel and Margaret West promptly offered to adopt one of the children and, at the age of nine, little Clarissa (Clara) Boehmer left her mother's and brothers' home in Jersey to become her Aunt Margaret's adoptive daughter in Manchester. Clara hated the move and resented being separated from her natural mother.

Aunt Margaret was also stepmother to Nathaniel's son by his first marriage, and the young New York man-about-town paid frequent visits. Fred Miller dazzled Clara Boehmer, and as a teenager she fell in love with her dashing older step-cousin. He, for his part, was amused when friends suggested that he might marry the little English cousin. But when his wild oats were sown, something about Clara attracted him seriously. And after he

CLARA BOEHMER MILLER, AGATHA'S MOTHER.

had proposed twice, he was accepted. In 1878, 32-year-old Fred married 24-year-old Clara and the two enjoyed 23 years of perfectly happy wedlock.

They were a living embodiment of the axiom that women like lazy men, since lazy men take time off to pay them attention. Fred, the epitome of rich idleness, was happy to put Clara first, leaving his children in the care of nurses, governesses and boarding schools. His business affairs were left in the hands of lawyers and financial advisers – who made a complete mess of them.

Agatha was five or six when it became apparent that the Millers' income was not meeting their expenditure. The classic upper-class Victorian way of saving money was to let the expensive English house full of servants and live for a spell on the continent where the cost of living was much lower. The Miller family moved to Pau, which is where we get early glimpses of Agatha as a little girl tired of always being youngest. It did not mean she was spoiled or cosseted. When she went with her father and big sister Madge on a mule trip up the mountains, they were critical when something upset her and she cried all the way home. Only her sensitive mother saw what the problem was: a well-meaning guide had trapped a bright butterfly and pinned it, still alive and fluttering, to the girl's hat. And she was too polite to alleviate her distress by overt complaint about a well-intentioned gesture.

Madge was a big sister who played frightening games that Agatha both enjoyed and dreaded. "The Elder Sister" was one. With a sinister, oily voice, Madge would pretend that she was a still older sister who was not well intentioned. This, coupled with Agatha's recurrent nightmare that a "gunman" – an eighteenth-century soldier with a musket – could undetectably replace familiar members of her family circle, seems to have provided background for a writer who would excel in creating characters who were not what they seemed to be.

Big brother Monty created another pattern that was to stay in Agatha's mind: the pattern of the lively, slangy, handsome young man. Although Monty was well embarked on his shaky career by proving a very poor scholar at Harrow, he had the young man's assured air of knowing, coupled with a young athlete's physical activity and courage. He was very superior to the sister 10 years his junior, and once, as a treat, took her out, in the dinghy he sailed around Torbay. Only once. She was persistently seasick – she would always be a rotten sailor – and he had little patience with little girls who "fed the fishes".

After the best part of a year in France and Jersey, the family came back to Torquay bringing a French nurse for Agatha to replace the English countrywomen who had tended her in early childhood. Agatha learned to speak fluent French without ever really being sure how the grammar worked, just as she believed she had learned to read simply by memorizing the names of shops and looking at the signs. Oddly for a writer, she was always happier manipulating figures than looking at the way words worked.

MONTY MILLER IN "TRUELOVE".

Ashfield

The family home which meant a great deal to Agatha was Ashfield, a comfortable early Victorian villa in the unfashionable Torre Mohun section of Torquay. She opened and closed her *Autobiography* with an invocation of it. It was, she said, her dear home, her nest, her place of safety. In old age, it was the place she dreamed of as "home", though it had long passed out of the family hands, been encroached upon by building development, and demolished.

ASHFIELD, AGATHA'S CHILDHOOD HOME.

Ashfield was Clara Miller's personal property. She fell in love with it and purchased it with her own recently inherited money when Fred sent her back from New York to Torquay to look for a home in England after Monty's birth. She did not consult Fred, but he accepted her choice, even though he thought they would not live there very long. The big, square stucco house had a massive conservatory to the front, and jalousied shutters, giving it the Riviera air. It stood in a large garden with a central bed of short-stem palms or aloes reinforcing the sub-tropical ambience. Agatha was more impressed by the mighty Wellingtonia; by the beech which was the garden's largest tree; by the two fir trees, one of which was Monty's for climbing, and the other held a secret bower-branch for Madge. As a little girl with long blonde hair and heavy-lidded eyes, dreamily playing imaginary games with an imaginary family of kittens, Agatha loved the ash wood at the foot of the garden; bowled her hoop round imaginary railway lines; and enjoyed the house rear's immediate proximity to country lanes and footpaths.

Indoors, an all-female staff marked the Millers as gentry, but not exceedingly rich. The very rich had butlers and footmen. The Millers had a cook, housemaids – who undertook the valeting of Fred's and Monty's clothes – and parlourmaids. The cook was "Mrs Rowe" – a Cornishwoman who ruled the kitchen absolutely. The senior maids were addressed by their surnames without prefixes; the younger ones by christian names, which the Millers firmly replaced with something suitably ordinary like Mary or Jane had the maids' parents chosen to dignify them above their station with appellations deemed more suitable for the classes than the masses – Muriel, say, or Cynthia.

And for Agatha there was always Nursie. An old countrywoman she loved, and whose constant memory ensured that for the rest of her life Agatha always described the heirs of Florence Nightingale as "hospital nurses", whether they worked in hospitals or not. Indeed, the concept of the children's nurse as an indispensable piece of domestic furniture was so strong in her that in *Sad Cypress* she allows the single word, "Morland," to convey the projected career of one character, although at least seventy per cent of her readership would be unlikely to have heard of Britain's top training school for nannies.

Agatha's confident assumption that servants would always be part of the household scene was modified by the end of her life to the observation that this was no longer the case as it had been in her childhood. She expressed considerable respect for them as professionals who did a job well, and herself believed that she could have made a living as a parlourmaid had circumstances required. Some of her characters – notably the admirable Lucy Eylesbarrow in *4.50 from Paddington* – show themselves quite capable of taking domestic employment without losing dignity or caste. Nonetheless in her own creative "Golden Age" of the 1920s and '30s Agatha sometimes mocked the uneducated "servant galisms" that *Punch* always found so funny. Fortunately for her sales, American anglophiles tend to treat the "Upstairs Downstairs" aspects of English life as endearing cultural traits, and not the class distinction which offends them in other areas.

Visitors to Ashfield in the early days included Rudyard Kipling and Henry James. Both would have easy introduction to Anglo-American homes: James as an American expatriate himself; Kipling as a refugee from Vermont where his rumbustious American brother-in-law Beatty Balestier had won local sympathy over a family quarrel. Although Kipling showed signs thereafter of mistrusting certain types of American, he still found the Torbay population of old ladies with lapdogs and respirators stifling, and would welcome the more relaxed and less genteel attitudes of a well-bred family from the New York aristocracy of business.

Like the Kiplings, the Millers gave family nicknames to people, things and places. In Ashfield, Agatha was given her first dog, a Yorkshire terrier named George Washington (by her father) and quickly reduced to "Tony". The battered old rocking-horse handed down from Madge to Monty to Agatha was called "Mathilde". The toy horse-and-pedal-dogcart was "Truelove". These toys lived among a jumble of tennis and croquet equipment in a little potting shed attached to a corner of the house and called, for some long forgotten reason, "the K.K." It all drifted back into Agatha's geriatric mind at the end of her life, when *The Postern of Fate* carried the hero couple she seemed most to identify with, Tommy and Tuppence Beresford, back to an Ashfield-like house with a K.K.-like conservatory, and a clue about K.K. or "Kai-Kai", which somehow Agatha forgot to explain or unravel.

FLORENCE NIGHTINGALE, THE ORIGINAL "HOSPITAL NURSE".

Reduced Circumstances

The idyllic phase of her childhood ended abruptly in 1901. Fred Miller, whose health had been shaky for some time, died suddenly. "An agreeable man", Agatha called him when looking back later in life. A cool but accurate assessment of the benign and self-indulgent figure who taught her arithmetic and imbued her with a lifelong pleasure in elementary mathematics; who called her "Agatha-Pagatha, my black hen (She lays eggs for gentlemen)", but who never put his children before his own pleasures when he wanted to travel. Agatha took his death more calmly than Clara, who was temporarily devastated.

AGATHA AS A CHILD.

The death of Fred revealed that his affairs were in a much worse state than anybody had realized. His trustees had invested badly and Fred had been incapable of sorting out the mess. There was little of Nathaniel Frary Miller's fortune left. Fred's step-mother who, being also Agatha's great-aunt, was always called "Auntie-Grannie", would receive a steady continuing income from H. B. Chaflin and Co. She was, after all, a partner's widow. Fred had contributed less to the firm. From the trust, Madge, Monty and Agatha would receive £100 a year apiece, and Clara would be given a small continuing income. But the days of entertaining distinguished visitors like Rudyard Kipling and Henry James with lavish dinners were over. Clara wanted to sell Ashfield and move to a smaller house in a cathedral town like Exeter. But the children protested vehemently at the idea of relinquishing the beloved family home, and Clara yielded to their pressure despite the financial burden.

Madge and Monty were not as intimately in need of Ashfield as Agatha. Monty had made unsuccessful attempts to start a career as an engineer; then joined the army during the Boer War, and finally gone to India with a commission in the East Surreys. Madge was about to marry James Watts, the son of an old schoolfriend of Clara. James's grandfather, Sir James, had founded an export firm in Manchester which traded grandly with the empire. He had built a magnificent over-decorated, over-furnished Victorian Gothic mansion, Abney Hall, which came to play an important part in Agatha's life and furnish the memory of the perfect traditional English Christmas, from stockings in bed in the morning to the candlelit tree at night, which she celebrated in the introduction to *The Adventure of the Christmas Pudding.*

Madge and James continued with the Miller tradition of letting relatives, servants or schools look after their children while they disported themselves. Every winter they went to the continent to skate. Every winter, Clara and Agatha stayed in their house, Cheadle Hall, and looked after their little boy, James. And they stayed on for the massive family Christmas at Abney which drew in the

AGATHA PAINTED BY "CONNAH" C.1894.

entire Watts family. Interestingly, its huge and much-loved Christmas dinner included one American tradition, opening with oyster soup.

If Abney gave Agatha familiarity with expensive country-house life in the north, Auntie-Grannie provided another comfortable base in London. On being widowed, the elderly Margaret Miller transported herself and her household effects to a large house in Ealing– still in those days more an outer than an inner suburb. Again, Agatha found an over-furnished Victorian house where she was a welcome little girl. Like her father, Auntie-Grannie played "Agatha-Pagatha, my black hen" with her, introducing a fascinating variant in which the hen was trussed and prepared for the table, only to be spared by transformation into a little girl after an elaborate ritual of knife-sharpening had built up a delightful suspense.

Auntie-Grannie was the rich granny. Granny B, who had married romantically for love, lived in poorer circumstances in Bayswater, and although Agatha's direct rather than collateral ancestress, had less acknowledged influence on the child than her sister. Granny B shopped for Auntie-Grannie at the Army and Navy Stores in Victoria Street, which both old ladies favoured. Auntie-Grannie tactfully slipped the carriage money and a little spare change to her sister when she came to Ealing to deliver the shopping. Agatha noted Auntie-Grannie's persistent unmalicious mistrust of other people's motives, and occasional gift of almost prophetic intuition, and remembered them as a basis for her later creation of Miss Marple. When Auntie-Grannie started to slip into Alzheimer's and came to live with Agatha and Clara in Torquay, Agatha took in the sad anxieties and irrational fears of the old and later incorporated them into successful pieces of writing.

Meanwhile, the child's education was overtly in that most upper-class of forms: "educated at home". But she was not the aristocratic pupil of hand-picked governesses and tutors. Clara gave her daughter a useful, but somewhat haphazard and unstructured education, with a lot of general reading. A few classes at a local school furthered her grasp of maths, but Agatha was never a regular pupil. The school fees that had secured Madge's and Monty's education were now beyond the family's resources. And while, quite correctly, Agatha never had any doubt that she was well-bred and a lady, she grew up to feel a little bit out of her depth when she married a man who would become a fellow of All Souls. She would later refer to herself as "a lowbrow" – a wildly inaccurate description. But one which derived from the reduced circumstances which denied her a recognizable formal education.

"AUNTIE-GRANNIE" IN OLD AGE.

Fun and Finishing School

Nan Watts, James's little sister, was a bridesmaid with Agatha at Madge's wedding. The two became fast friends for life. Agatha taught Nan the taste for drinking rich, full cream by the cupful, sometimes abstemiously thinning it with just a little milk. This would be one of Agatha's lifetime indulgences. She wisely declined ever to acquire the taste for alcohol – except in cooking – and drank her cream where others would stimulate themselves with strong drink. Equally wisely, in later life she did not wish this foible on her fictional characters, but kept them smartly up-to-date with the "cocktail habit" (or, for Poirot, *siropes*). And although herself a non-smoker who detested the smell of tobacco smoke, she gave Poirot his very small Belgian cigarettes as one of his simple trade marks. She had no compunction about describing herself as "greedy" – another trait her characters were spared – though she lamented her fate when her metabolism caught up with her and she turned into a fat old lady with piano legs.

She had healthier juvenile pastimes. She went swimming – a lifelong passion – and willingly walked three miles to her favourite beach. Walking was another pleasure, though by the time she reached her twenties she was unwilling to progress very far uphill. She rode side-saddle, which she always felt to be elegant as well as comfortable, and which probably explains why she was not seen as a particularly good horsewoman once riding astride became possible for ladies.

The long dresses that dictated side-saddle riding, coupled with tailored jackets and large ornate hats, gave Edwardian teenagers the look of very mature young ladies. Agatha and the three Lucy girls, on holiday from Warwickshire with their older brother Reggie, went roller skating on the pier. And very serious and demure they all looked, holding hands in a long line. With Dr Huxley's five daughters, she performed in an all-female amateur production of *The Yeomen of the Guard*. She was a great hit, singing a man's role in what she later recognized as a breathy soprano. And thereafter, singing was the one form of public appearance she could manage without crippling shyness. With the Huxleys, she put on amateur theatricals well into her early twenties. Her father had produced amateur plays in Torquay. She herself contributed to scripting lively and facetious tomfoolery like *The Blue-Beard of Un-Happiness*, an Arabian Nights-based skit punning on Maurice Maeterlinck's idealist futurist drama *The Bluebird of Happiness*.

AGATHA (CENTRE) WITH THE LUCY GIRLS AND THEIR BROTHER REGGIE, ROLLER SKATING IN TORQUAY.

Madge remained a teasingly friendly elder sister, too, encouraging her to join in certain sorts of mischief that belie any notion of pre-World War One young married ladies as stuffy. When Madge dressed up as a cricketer in cap and breeches to come down to dinner, she persuaded young Agatha to bundle herself into shapeless black clothes and belch her way politely through the meal in the guise of "a Turkish lady."

Music was the one area in which Agatha was always taught professionally. Her first piano tutor was German Fräulein Üder. Her next was a Miss Trotter. When Clara decided that Agatha should go to Paris and live *en pension* to improve her French and undergo general "finishing" in the company of other young Englishwomen on the continent, her musical education was again treated very seriously compared with the rather scrappy training in French culture and grammar, dancing, deportment and general "accomplishments" that prepared the young ladies at Mlle Cabernet's, at Les Marroniers in Auteuil, and finally at Miss Dryden's English finishing school back in Paris. Agatha's singing master, M. Boue, was one of the best in Paris, and corrected her breathiness. Her piano instructor was an excellent Austrian teacher called Charles Fürster. Active musicianship as a concert pianist seems to have been the only way in which Agatha ever contemplated making her own living. It was a wrench to abandon the hope when she performed before a visitor and broke down with stage-fright. And Herr Furster told her frankly (when she asked) that he did not think her temperament would ever fit her for public performance.

She seems to have valued his honesty rather than resenting his criticism. Even in adolescence, Agatha showed considerable courage in facing reality. From this time, too, we might date the mild tendency to favour things German and Austrian over things French that appears in her work. Although she had spoken French since she was a child in Pau, she never really mastered its written grammar or wrote with very much sympathy about France. And living in a period when the Germanophile Conan Doyle could be persuaded by war to see Germans as bullet-headed militaristic huns, Agatha always respected German patriots. Could this be because her first and last piano teachers were German and Austrian? Or because as a naturally musical person she could never value the nation that gave us Fauré, Debussy and Ravel above the majestic musical race that produced Bach and Handel, Haydn and Mozart, Beethoven and Schubert, Wagner, Mahler and Bruckner?

JOSEPH HAYDN.

Cairo

The goal of finishing a young lady was to prepare her for her debut: her "coming-out" as an adult onto the marriage market. There were hardly any other careers open to upper-class Edwardian ladies.

The London debutante season, however, was expensive. Presentation at court was the central ceremony. Rounds of parties and dances deliberately threw well-chaperoned young ladies and gentlemen together to encourage them to contract suitable engagements within their own upper class circles. Certain formal sporting occasions were *de rigeur*: Royal Ascot, the Eton and Harrow cricket match, Henley Regatta, and possibly Oxford eights week and Cambridge May eights. The Millers were not rich enough to afford the London season. Madge's coming-out had been staged in less expensive New York. Agatha's was yet more exotic. In 1910 she went with Clara to Cairo.

In part this was justified by Clara's health. She had suffered a number of minor heart attacks since Fred's death, and Agatha, who became very close to her mother, had moved into a bedroom next to hers to administer sal volatile or brandy during the night if necessary. A rest in a warm climate in an appropriate part of the empire might be prescribed for the ailing who could afford it. And Mrs Miller took her daughter to the British protectorate to "come out" among the army officers at reduced cost.

Tutankamun's tomb had not yet been discovered, but there were still fascinating antiquities in the Cairo museum. Agatha was not interested. Nor was she tempted by the offer of a cruise down the Nile to see the great temples of Luxor and Karnak. The future author of *Death on the Nile* and an ambitious play about the

AGATHA RIDING HER DONKEY SIDE SADDLE IN EGYPT.

pharaoh Akhnaton took no precocious interest in Egyptology when she was seventeen. She visited the pyramids and the Sphinx, and looked very fetching riding her donkey side-saddle with a parasol across her knees. And that was enough for her.

She had come to Cairo to enjoy the social scene. She went to at least three dances a week for three months. She went on picnics with young officers. She watched polo matches. She sat on camp stools to watch military reviews and tame manoeuvres. She was fascinated by clothes. She had ball gowns made for her by Levantine dressmakers. A piece of exquisite blue taffeta from Grannie B's remnant chest made a beautiful gown. But the fabric was so old it split up the skirt, under the sleeve and round the neck while Agatha was dancing, and she had to retire to the ladies' cloakroom in a hurry. Fifty years later she still remembered the materials from which her Egyptian finery had been crafted: she remembered, too, that all the young girls longed for black dresses, which they felt would make them look mature. And their mothers stoutly resisted letting them have such slinky allure.

Agatha was quite open about the skill she acquired in Cairo. She learned to flirt. She was proud of it as a necessary social acquisition. Not for her any man-hating feminism. She had no interest in votes for women. Politics was a male preserve. A girl's duty was to listen with every appearance of awestruck admiration while a young man prated on about the Irish question or the urgent need for eight more Dreadnoughts or (the ultimate boring topic of the day) the economics of bi-metallism, the chaos caused by the USA's issue of both gold and silver dollars which never maintained an exactly equal value as they were influenced by the shifting market prices of precious metals.

Agatha was better at flirtation by listening than flirtation by teasing. One Captain of Rifles with whom she danced restored her to Clara with the words, "Here's your daughter. She has learnt to dance. In fact she dances beautifully. You had better try to teach her to talk now." As he was engaged to some one else, Agatha's tongue-tied shyness might have been seen as suitable maiden modesty. But she remembered all her life this public advertisement of her lack of conversation. Like the split ballgown, it was in the end useful training in meeting social adversity with ladylike calm. She became a quiet conversationalist with strangers and a sparkling companion with intimates.

And with children. Back in England, Madge and James had a little boy, and Agatha adored her nephew Jack. She would always enjoy small boys, becoming a perfect grandmother in middle age. She was merrily tolerant of Jack's high spirits, and amused by his cheek when he she called him a rascal and he called her a lady rascal; then a lady elephant when she carried him; and finally a lady swan. By the time she attributed this piece of memory to her fictional alter ego, Mrs Ariadne Oliver, she might have had her doubts about being called an elephant, given her considerable bulk in old age. But she was remarkably confident about her good looks as a young woman. The large-boned, oval-faced, fair-haired, blue-eyed Edwardian ideal was one she matched. Although her autobiographical novel *Unfinished Portrait* showed the heroine using fabric "plumpers" to compensate for an undeveloped bosom, Agatha took an unusual satisfaction in her appearance, and would always expect heroic men and handsome women to be tall, like her.

OPPOSITE: HOLLYWOOD PUTS ANGELA LANSBURY ASTRIDE IN *DEATH ON THE NILE*.

Courted

Her adolescent gaucherie smoothed away, Agatha returned to find her fate in England. Her fate, she had no doubt, would be a suitable husband. She enjoyed her young unmarried life "on the prowl", being courted by unmarried officers. Her account of it in her *Autobiography* suggests a world less aristocratic and fashionable than Barbara Cartland's, but also less sugary and pink-hazed. Agatha hugely enjoyed being a young woman of the leisure classes in an age when the marriage market was open and above board, and young men were easily carried away into making romantic proposals.

Agatha received several, and took proper pride in them. One, however, was as embarrassing as Mr Elton's proposal to Emma. A man who had danced completely unwanted attendance on her at a weekend party drove her to the station; then leaped into her railway compartment and demanded that she marry him. He refused to leave, although he was flatly rejected. And there followed a long and tense journey to London in a corridorless train.

The social round of the leisure classes included lots of games. Agatha was indifferent as an archer, a billiards player, a tennis player, a golfer, and a croquet player. There were visits to the races, and bridge parties in the evenings. Since matrimony was expected to give young woman financial security, there was neither false modesty nor snobbery about money. It was expected that young subalterns could not marry on their pay. If they had no private means, they must wait for promotion unless they had the luck to captivate a girl with a personal fortune. But unmarried girls living with their parents were usually kept on narrow dress allowances, so the relatively poor like Agatha were not humiliated. Hostesses prevented girls from gambling and covered their expenses.

A SPIRITUALIST SEANCE. ONE OF THE INTERESTS OF AGATHA'S GENERATION WHICH SHE ONLY SHARED UP TO A POINT.

The proprieties were observed with some curious rules. It was all right for a young man to take a girl golfing or walking unchaperoned, but not to take her to tea in a hotel. In general, pre-marital chastity was observed by the girls, and young men could be deeply embarrassed if they came across young women who wanted unlicensed bedroom romps. By the end of her life, Agatha felt convinced that the self-controlled waiting for sex of her youth was preferable to the earnest pursuit of sex as though it were an examinable academic exercise which she observed in young people of the 1960s. It was taken for granted, of course, that young men would sow their wild oats with *demi-mondaines* or older married women.

Agatha fell hopelessly and silently in love twice with tall young men who could not afford to propose to her. She reached three "understandings" as the delicate phase before formal engagement was then called, one with a man fifteen years older who wrote beautiful love letters, but had nothing to talk about except his devotion when they were together. Though her family thought him marvelously suitable in every way, Agatha broke off the understanding with relief after Clara had proposed a six months' separation for her to come to a decision. The second, with naval lieutenant Wilfred Pirie, had the complete approval of the young people's mothers: old family friends since the days of economical living in France. Agatha had plenty to talk about with Wilfred. Only he became fascinated by theosophy and spiritualist mediums. Agatha had a low tolerance for tosh, and broke off the understanding when he went to South America on an Inca treasure hunting expedition.

The third was the most important. The Lucy girls' older brother Reggie was an army major, posted to the far east. He was gentle and unhurried, and although the Lucys sometimes irritated Agatha by their dilatory tendency to miss trains and hold picnics in the wrong places, she felt in later life that he would probably have made a perfect husband. But he refused to rush her; insisted that she take the two years of his next tour of duty to "look around her" and see if she could find some one better. And as she later realized, this lack of romance and jealousy left her dissatisfied.

AGATHA AND ARCHIE CHRISTIE.

She had started the habit of observing herself and others in love with considerable insight. Her later books would be studded with wise and homely observations on love and marriage. She saw that young men rendered sheepish by devotion were singularly unattractive unless one reciprocated the interest. She remarked that men saw women as potential bed partners and often fell in love at first sight; women "tried on" men as potential husbands, and took a little longer. She would observe that men who married for money usually made good and grateful husbands, whereas King Cophetuas who raised poor beggarmaids to their wealth and status were apt to become annoyed if they didn't get back constant adulation. She noted that most jealous wives were not actually being deceived, but were suffering from the lack of passion in their marriages, because men had the extraordinary habit of marrying for generous reasons that had nothing to do with actually being in love. But even justified jealousy was a price worth paying to marry a man one adored passionately for life. She came to know passion herself, and ultimately mistrust it. But that was because of Archie.

Archie

COLONEL ARCHIE CHRISTIE.

Agatha met the young Lieutenant of Artillery at a dance at a friend's house. He was stationed at Exeter. He appealed to her sense of adventure, for he wanted to join the Royal Flying Corps as soon as he could. Agatha adored the nascent age of mechanical speed. She loved being driven fast in cars – still the rare toys of the rich – and had persuaded Clara to pay the expensive charge of £5 for her to take a five-minute joy-ride in a light aeroplane. In the days of everyday crashes, this took courage on the part of mother and daughter. But Agatha loved swooping through the sky, strapped in the open cockpit. In old age she regretted the boredom of motionless droning across a flat landscape in commercial jets.

Archie Christie was practical. He foresaw the role of planes in war. He anticipated quick promotion in a new service. He had only his pay to live on, and needed to rise fast.

But he was smitten by the tall, fair-haired girl with blue eyes. A few days later he rode his motor-bike over to Torquay and dropped in at Ashfield on a flimsy pretext. Agatha was out, practising the new parlour trick of waltzing up and down staircases with a neighbour. A telephone call from Clara summoned her home. Mrs Miller did not like being left to entertain Agatha's conquests, and it was a pink-faced and slightly embarrassed Archie Christie who was sitting tight and politely declining to leave until Agatha arrived.

He stayed for a meal and he won Agatha's heart. Here was a man with the passionate precipitancy she missed in cautious Reggie. A man who wouldn't wait, but insisted they must marry at once. A man who bounced and banged across pot-holed roads on a motorbike. Agatha was quite sure that she really had found the man for her.

Clara threw cold water on the proposal. What had Archie got to live on beyond his pay, she asked? Agatha had nothing but the annual £100 she inherited. Nor were there any great expectations. The mighty firm of H.B. Chaflin had itself crashed, ruined by ambitious under-capitalized expansion. Auntie-Grannie's investment in the firm had been saved by the wise and discreet advice of an older partner who, without telling her why, got her to shift her money out in time. Clara had her £300 a year benevolently continued out of his own pocket by another director. Agatha and Madge both handed over much of their own £100 a year to help Clara stay in Ashfield. So was there enough to live on?

Shamefacedly, Archie had to confess there was not.

There was another quiet objection the Millers held against the Christies. One of Hercule Poirot's best rare jokes was the observation that when one Englishman calls another a "*pukka sahib*" it means they went to the same sort of schools. But this did not just mean public schools (i.e. private boarding schools) as against "Board Schools" (local authority maintained day schools). Within the Headmaster's Conference listing the officially approved "Public Schools" there was a great range running from the College of the Blessed Virgin Mary at Eton to the Wesleyan Middle-Class School for Cornwall. And those two were not "the same sort of schools". Eton and Harrow probably recognized Winchester as *pukka*. Shrewsbury, Rugby and Westminster considered they should be in the top sector. The rest fell into an uncertain and competitive pecking order. Archie had been head boy of Clifton, the Bristol public school whose unique and well-intentioned inclusion of a special boarding house catering to Jewish dietary and religious laws neither suppressed anti-Semitic attitudes among the boys nor won the school social prestige outside Jewish circles. Monty Miller was an Old Harrovian. Madge went to the school that became Roedean. In due course Agatha would send her daughter to Benenden, while her grandson went to Eton. Frankly, in Clara and Madge's eyes, Archie Christie and his brother Campbell were not really *pukka*.

Agatha, bless her, was not moved by this sort of silliness. Indeed, a touch of opposition may well have increased the romance for her. Certainly she completely set aside her hard-headed knowledge that Grannie Boehmer, who married a poor young officer for love, ended her days in mildly straitened circumstances, while Auntie-Grannie, who married an older man with money, lived a comfortably independent life until increasing blindness forced her to come to Ashfield, where her income was a welcome addition to the housekeeping and her daughter could look after her. Agatha wrote to Reggie Lucy, breaking off their understanding (to his mild surprise and definite regret). She made her own quite definite understanding with Archie. And she entered on the most passionate relationship of her life.

It had the tempestuousness of passion-based romance. They did not always see eye to eye about Archie's occasional reckless expenditure on her. At different times one or the other would feel they *must* go their own way to formal engagement and marriage. But with war looming, Agatha was definitely committed to her chosen Mr Right.

ETON: A *PUKKA* PUBLIC SCHOOL.

World War One

For Archie and Agatha, as for so many other young couples, war changed everything. The financial prudence of a long engagement looked pettifogging when set against the risk of death without matrimony. Archie had joined the Royal Flying Corps and was flying planes at the front. Agatha, even though she later thought the assassination in Sarajevo brought about an unexpected catastrophe, had been sufficiently driven by war clouds to take classes in first aid and bandaging before the war broke out. When Torquay Town Hall was turned into a hospital, she became, first a ward maid, and then, as the elderly matrons who were at first preferred for nursing proved too squeamish, a V.A.D. (Volunteer Aid Detachment nurse).

TORQUAY PAVILION PARADE TODAY.

Archie, at first sure he would be killed in the first wave of fliers at the front, refused to consider marriage. Agatha wanted it. When he came home on leave before Christmas they had one further row about an expensive dressing-case he had bought her and which she wanted him to return. And then he changed his mind abruptly, decided they must marry by licence on Christmas Eve, and Agatha, after demurring, consented.

Only Archie's stepfather gave them his blessing. Archie's mother took to her bed asking how they could do this to her. Madge berated Agatha for putting Clara's weak heart at risk. But quietly, with no white dress, no wedding party or breakfast, the wedding took place at Clifton, and the young couple went down to Torquay for Christmas Day, where all was forgiven and they enjoyed the somewhat febrile happiness of those who knew active service lay between them and their future.

Archie was extremely brave, mentioned in dispatches four times; awarded the CMG and DFC, as well as the Order of St Stanislaus from the Czarist government. A typical gruffly modest Englishman he insisted that only the first mention in dispatches was worth anything. And a young man of his time, he tried to laugh off the traumatic experiences of front line combat, and refused to talk about the War. Agatha, by contrast, felt that exposure to casualties and the bedpans and pus and urine inseparable from nursing was making her more serious. They enjoyed his rare leaves, particularly one holiday in the New Forest. But temperamentally and unwittingly they were growing in different directions, and probably not quite in the ways Agatha imagined. Although she felt herself to have become more grave and sensible while Archie became more frivolous and unwilling to talk seriously, he probably masked an underlying gravity, while she was quietly but positively enjoying the experience of being something more than an elegant offering for sacrifice on the altar of economically secure matrimony. For some time their shared youthful adventurousness bridged this gulf. But ultimately it would pull them apart.

The most important thing to happen to Agatha during the war was her transfer from nursing to the dispensary. She learned basic chemistry and blew up a Cona coffee maker trying to carry out the Marsh test for arsenic. She was accredited by Apothecaries' Hall and came to find pharmacy boring in the long run. But she had gained some esoteric knowledge: how the action of instant poisons might be delayed; which poisons produced unfamiliar symptoms; what wrongly used herbs or medicines might prove poisonous. And this came to the forefront of her mind when she recalled a pre-war bet with Madge.

Since 1910, both sisters had written occasional short stories for magazines. Indeed, had not marriage and motherhood demanded Madge's time and attention, she might have become as notable a writer as Agatha. She used the pseudonym "Mack Miller", and Agatha was following in her footsteps when she, too, started sending stories to magazines under the pseudonym "Daniel Miller". Although she had long contributed occasional rather twee poems to *Poetry Review,* Agatha only ventured into prose when Clara suggested that writing a story might profitably pass a dull afternoon.

In 1911, Madge and Agatha were discussing the detective fiction both enjoyed (Sherlock Holmes, Arsène Lupin, and an imaginative new detective called Rouletabille). When Agatha said she would like to write a detective novel, Madge bet her she couldn't as it would be too difficult to plot. In 1917, bored with dispensing tonics and smelly salves, Agatha started putting her newfound knowledge of poisons to good use by writing a whodunnit in her spare time. To give her detective as much originality as Rouletabille, she decided to make him a Belgian refugee: there were several in Tor parish. She made him a rather vain and conceited retired police inspector; a man with a tremendous brain who boasted of his "little grey cells"; a precisian fuss-budget who liked everything absolutely neat and tidy and arranged symmetrically. When she found herself getting stuck with the plot, Clara advised her to use her fortnight's holiday to finish it in a hotel on Dartmoor. Agatha loved Dartmoor, and spent a profitable two weeks near Chagford, walking on the moors and completing *The Mystery at Styles.* She sent it to four publishers who all rejected it. And she virtually forgot about it when the fifth, John Lane, simply did not acknowledge it. For in 1918 Archie was transferred from the front to the War Office, and soon after that the War came to an end. Agatha became a young housewife and, to her great delight, a mother.

HOLMES AND WATSON.

BELGIAN POLICE OFFICERS.

Early Married Years

THE END OF THE GREAT WAR.

Archie was not wounded. But he was not unscathed. Flying had exposed his tendency to crippling sinusitis, for which reason he was sent back to his honourable desk job in Whitehall. He also suffered from chronic nervous dyspepsia, and was likely to be laid low by Agatha's best culinary efforts, preferring stodgy treacle puddings.

While the war lasted they enjoyed the services of his batman, a first-class "gentleman's gentleman" who kept their tiny flat perfect. When hostilities ended and the batman was demobbed, he was replaced by an incompetent soldier who smeared surfaces rather than cleaning them. But still, as they were always to do, the young couple enjoyed the first of the two great pre-war benefits which Agatha noted sadly had virtually disappeared by the end of her life. They had servants in the home.

They had lost the other benefit leisure. Working for a living was an inevitability. Promotion in the RFC proved no faster than in the Artillery. So although a colonel and a war hero, Archie started looking around for "something in the City". He was lucky enough to find a niche in a stockbroking firm, luckier still that he proved good at the work, and that his employer, did not know that the Christies looked down on him as "fat and very yellow," their typical epithets for Jewish businessmen. A comfortable salary was necessary. While Archie was still in the Air Ministry Agatha felt too embarrassed to take up with her old friend Nan Watts, now Mrs Pollock and living in London. The Christies simply couldn't afford to entertain the Pollocks as well as they would be entertained.

Very soon after the Armistice, Agatha found herself pregnant. Archie wanted the baby to be a girl. A boy, he feared, would make him feel displaced and jealous: an interestingly advanced psychological prediction from a man who tends to be described by Agatha's admirers as a pretty conventional cold fish of a soldier turned stockbroker. Agatha went to Ashfield to give birth to Rosalind who, she was delighted to find, was born with thick black hair and the Red Indian look newborns may have as an alternative to the fair, bald, Winston Churchill look. And starting a pattern she would follow throughout Rosalind's childhood, Agatha left her offspring in other people's care (Clara's and the nurse-midwife's) and went back to London to find a larger unfurnished flat, and engage a nursemaid and general maid.

The following year, the public Agatha Christie was born. Out of the blue John Lane wrote accepting *The Mysterious Affair at Styles*, which had got pushed to the back of a drawer in his Bodley Head publishing office and forgotten. Lane's reader wanted the last chapter rewritten to removing an unconvincing court scene as the denouement, and so probably inspired that recurrent Christiean moment when Poirot gathers all the suspects in one room and expounds the truth. Lane offered Agatha a typical first contract, taking an ungenerous option on her next five books. Agatha accepted it with a first-time author's typical unawareness that she might regret it if her work was successful. The white goateed publisher of Oscar Wilde and *The Yellow Book* seems a strange godparent for Hercule Poirot and Tommy and Tuppence. But Lane had never much liked his naughty nineties authors, refusing to let Wilde contribute to *The Yellow Book*, and sacking Beardsley as its art editor when his designs were too obviously erotic.

Two further books ensured that Agatha Christie was a fixture on the roster of crime and adventure fiction writers. *The Secret Adversary* introduced Tommy and Tuppence Beresford. *Murder on the Links* firmly established Poirot and, Agatha hoped, dispensed with the unnecessary stereotyped conventional "Watson" by marrying Captain Hastings off. But serialization of the novel attracted further editorial attention, and Agatha was invited to write more short stories featuring Poirot. These were most easily done retaining the familiar voice of Hastings and the familiar Scotland Yard foil, Inspector Japp, and so Agatha found herself more or less committed to a detective hero whose foibles increasingly irritated her as his national characteristics evaded her (according to letters from readers), and whom she could not improve by maturing him, since he was already elderly. On the credit side, she thoroughly mastered writing in a convincing masculine voice, and could subsequently use other male narrators without their sounding as wooden as Hastings or in any way strained.

OSCAR WILDE AND (ABOVE) POIROT, BOTH OF WHOM WERE ASSOCIATED WITH JOHN LANE.

But before *Murder on the Links* was published Archie received a challenging offer. A former master at Clifton, Major E.A. Belcher, had discovered an unsuspected talent for publicity – especially self-advertisement – and become Controller of Potato Supplies during the war. Now he had got himself put in charge of pre-publicizing and organizing the planned Empire Exhibition at Wembley, and proposed to tour the world setting things up. He invited Archie to come as his assistant. The adventure appealed to Archie, as did the possibility of a temporary break from his City job which, he suspected, was shadily placing him in directorships of companies that were intended to fail. He thought Agatha could travel with him for the year on the £1000 Belcher offered.

Round THE World WITH Major Belcher

LEFT TO RIGHT: MAJOR BELCHER'S SECRETARY BATES, BELCHER, ARCHIE, AGATHA.

Few incidents mark more clearly the adventurousness shared by Archie and Agatha. There was little certainty that his job would be held open for him on his return. The finance for the year would be rather tight. But visiting southern Africa and the Pacific, with a holiday in Hawaii before going on to Canada, was an opportunity they would not miss. Rosalind and her nursemaid were complacently handed over to relatives, Clara and Madge (the latter now known in the family as "Punkie"). Madge didn't object to having the child dumped on her. She did, however, think that Agatha should have made an effort to stay at home and greet their brother Monty who was now coming back in ill health from Africa, where a pre-war attempt to set up a cargo boat on Lake Victoria had failed because of the outbreak of war, and a postwar stretch as a white hunter ended with an injury festering and fever threatening his life. Agatha determinedly went her and Archie's chosen way.

The Trade Mission quickly proved more difficult than they anticipated. Agatha was miserably seasick throughout the Bay of Biscay. Belcher turned out to be mercurial. His vaunted organizational skills, Agatha felt, consisted of tearing apart an existing organization with the intention of rebuilding it perfectly from top to bottom. Only he was hopeless at the rebuilding. He was bad tempered with his staff when he didn't get obsequious attention and adulation. His secretary, a very young and thin man called Bates with a dread of snakes, a sinister face, and an unblemished innocence, was the principal victim of Belcher's explosions, what the Christies called his outbreaks of "Wild Man".

But they enjoyed South Africa. Archie loved swimming as much as Agatha, and the two of them enthusiastically took up the new sport of surfing. Agatha also enjoyed a lecture in Capetown on cave paintings and archaeological discoveries. She liked Durban, too, which reminded her of Torquay.

The Rand was more difficult. Belcher was outraged that the anti-imperialist Afrikaaner nationalist politician Hertzog refused to meet him. He sacked Bates on the spot – relenting only on condition that the secretary stayed out of his sight thereafter – on discovering that a pamphlet which should have been translated into Afrikaans had been rendered in High Dutch. And while the party was there, the "Rand Rebellion" took place, a general strike called by white unions when mine owners tried to hold wages down by increasing the employment of

ARCHIE WITH SURF BOARD.

cheaper black labour. When the strikers grew violent the government called in troops and declared that it was an attempt at revolution fomented by the Third International, to which some of the strike leaders belonged. They executed some Communists, and Agatha believed the government's reactionary vapouring, which found its way into an unconvincing episode in her next novel.

The Mission had hoped go to India and Ceylon. But the monsoon was against them, and Australia and New Zealand were substituted after Agatha and Archie had visited Rhodesia. Before leaving the continent, Agatha made a large collection of African wooden animals and pokerwork, decades before Kamba carving became a staple of airport art.

Australia and New Zealand were pleasant. Agatha visited a huge ranch in the bush at Coochin Coochin where the active Bell sisters reminded her of her outgoing friends the Lucys. New Zealand, she felt all her life, was the most beautiful country she ever visited, and she much regretted never getting back in the spring to see the *rata* in bloom. The increasingly difficult Belcher stayed in New Zealand with friends while the Christies went on for their long-anticipated holiday month in Honolulu.

Surfing proved more exciting but more exacting than it had been in South Africa. They cut their feet on coral and burned and blistered their backs in the midday sun. Agatha's expensive silk bathing costume split from top to bottom. But surviving the embarrassment, she was delighted by the much smaller and more becoming wool one she bought in Honolulu. It all proved far more expensive than they had expected. With the result that economies were in force when they visited Canada, with Belcher rudely complaining about their having taken the holiday he had agreed to.

Agatha took to eating everything available at the hotel breakfasts, and then foregoing later meals unless she was invited out. And it was arranged that she should stay in New York with her father's sister Cassie while Archie and Belcher toured Newfoundland and Nova Scotia. Archie, unfortunately, came down with really severe sinus problems complicated by bronchitis after visiting grain silos in Winnipeg. Belcher was furious with him for daring to be ill. Agatha was relieved to be rescued from kind Aunt Cassie, who took her everywhere, introduced her to rich Morgan relations-in-law, but would not let her go on the streets alone. As she was now over 30, Agatha felt like caged bird after a while.

On the voyage back, Agatha's seasickness held off long enough to let her and Belcher win the ship's bridge tournament. But the Christies swore that they would never speak to the unpredictable and explosive ex-schoolmaster again.

AGATHA WITH SURF BOARD.

If at First You Don't Succeed...

The return home seemed a little less than triumphant. Archie's job had gone to a younger man, and the bullish postwar City market had been succeeded by a bearish phase. There didn't seem to be any openings for a man in his thirties with a good war record, but limited business experience. The marriage didn't seem to work as a support in adversity. Archie's increasing depression led him to suggest that it might be better for Agatha to spend more time with Clara and Madge, since she never seemed to be grave or gay at the right times for him.

AGATHA AT THE TIME OF HER FIRST SUCCESS.

But mother and sister were not entirely perfect companions, either. They felt no resentment about having taken charge of Rosalind for a year. But they and Rosalind recognized a resulting bond which Agatha could only weaken, not properly replace.

"Where's Auntie Punkie?" had been Rosalind's off-putting challenge when Agatha returned to claim her daughter. And Auntie Punkie had no hesitation about telling Agatha what Rosalind should be wearing and eating. Thereafter a succession of mostly unsatisfactory nursemaids didn't help. Nor did Agatha's need to shut herself away and write. She was laying the foundations for an awkward relationship with her daughter. Both her *Autobiography* and her play and novel *A Daughter's a Daughter* evince intense unease about the mother-daughter relationship. Not obvious guilt. But a feeling of something missing. Agatha had experienced parenting by a couple who never spared their own pleasures in their children's interest. She had lived into a time when offspring were supposed to engage a mother's undivided attention and devotion for some years. And this, she simply could not give. Archie, adoring his daughter but knowing that men had to work to support their families, felt none of his wife's misgivings about time spent apart from her.

Rosalind's Uncle Monty was another emotional problem Agatha had not fully shared, although she had

offered money to help with the native servant he brought back from Africa with him – to the consternation of Clara's elderly servants who wanted to give notice rather than work with a black man in the house. Worse than the native servant was Monty's own habit of firing pistols out of his bedroom window, "to keep his hand in". When he decided it was funny to scare a neighbour by shooting behind her – an incident Agatha later exploited in fiction – enough was clearly enough. The native servant went back to Africa. And Monty was packed off to a cottage on Dartmoor with a nurse-housekeeper whom he charmed into devoted subjection.

Even Agatha's increasingly successful fiction had a downside. The Inland Revenue wrote asking why she had made no return on her literary earnings. Agatha had never thought of them as taxable income. She assumed that the small sums were "casual profits" that need not be declared. At this stage she and the tax authorities could afford to be good humoured. But it was an omen of serious injustice to come.

On the positive side, she thoroughly enjoyed Madge's success with a play about the great Victorian fraud, the Tichborne Claimant, which enjoyed a short run in the West End. Both sisters were enjoying reflected glory from each other's growing literary prestige, and Agatha took immense and prophetic pleasure from going backstage and meeting the actors in a major West End theatre.

THE TICHBORNE CASE: THE GREAT VICTORIAN IMPOSTURE WHICH MADGE MILLER DRAMATIZED SUCCESSFULLY.

And things started to look up for Archie, who found work, first in a firm so shady that he knew he would have to be careful not to be left with any legal responsibilities for their dubious dealings, and then at last with an old war friend who gave him security and worthwhile business responsibility. As became a rising businessman, he became a keen golfer. And knowing that Agatha liked the country, he proposed that they take a flat in the developing Berkshire area of Sunningdale. Stockbrokers' suburbia, with its expanding golf courses, was not Agatha's idea of a rural retreat. But she made no complaint as they moved, first into a large flat in a house divided into four equal flats – a setting she would reproduce in Miss Marple's "Case of the Perfect Maid" – and then into a newish modern house that she found as unpleasantly impersonal as a hotel. The only thing really in its favour was a good garden for Rosalind to play in.

The neighbourhood thought the house unlucky. Previous owners had lost their money or suffered broken marriages. The Christies tried to take the curse off by renaming it Styles, after Agatha's first success. Yet that house of murder and conspiracy could hardly have been a good omen.

On the credit side, their friendship with Belcher miraculously revived. He proved good company when they were not his fellow-travelling employees. Agatha agreed to his ebullient demand that she put him in a detective novel as the villain, and he became "Sir Eustace Pedler" of *The Man in the Brown Suit.* Serialized as *Anne's Adventure*, the novel brought Agatha a windfall of £500. That really was good money at the time, and her initial feeling was that it should be put aside for a rainy day. But Archie had a different idea.

THE MAN IN THE BROWN SUIT: THE THRILLER MEETING MAJOR BELCHER'S DEMAND THAT HE BE PORTRAYED AS A VILLAIN.

Crises

A BULL-NOSE MORRIS COWLEY: THE MAKE OF AGATHA'S FIRST CAR.

Archie's idea was that rather than putting the money into savings, or buying a few little treats like a fairy cycle for Rosalind, they should buy a car and Agatha should learn to drive it. This was extravagant recklessness at first sight. But he had summed her up rightly. She loved driving her bull-nose Morris Cowley and the sense of freedom it brought.

Only she'd had one other idea about the extra money before accepting the car proposal. She had wondered whether they might not have a second child. And too easily accepted Archie's dismissal of the suggestion. The marriage was not rooting itself in central family love.

This was not apparent to Agatha, who had at last solved her nursemaid problem. Advertising for a combined nurse and secretary, she found the young daughter of a Scottish manse, Charlotte "Carlo" Fisher. Carlo proved a treasure. She corrected Rosalind's manners, which had gone to pot under the previous dispensation, settled to handling Agatha's business correspondence and became a real friend.

It should not have been a crisis in 1926 when *Who Killed Roger Ackroyd?* became more of a talking point than any of Agatha's previous books. But since her central device was controversial, some reviewers baldly called the book a disappointment in which she had "cheated". At this stage, however, Agatha was unafraid of publicity. When the *Daily Sketch* commissioned a series of Poirot stories, she let their reporter and cameraman come to Styles and take pictures of her with Rosalind and her wooden African animals.

It was obviously critical that the Christies were overspending their income. Archie was a little too sanguine about his good new job and Agatha's newfound ability to turn a few more pennies with a short story whenever some little addition to the house was needed. It was clear they would have to draw in their horns a bit. They decided to rent Styles, while Agatha went to Ashfield and Archie stayed in his club. The money saved should put them back in credit and pay for a holiday in Alassio at the end of the summer.

The visit to Ashfield should have come as something of a relief. Archie's increasing passion for golf meant that husband and wife spent very little time together, and Agatha was becoming very bored with suburban life, which was not to her taste. But at Ashfield Clara's health was declining fast. And when she suddenly died, Agatha realized how much she had meant to her and was disconsolate, rather as Clara herself had been on Fred's death. Archie was not appropriately sympathetic. He wanted his wife to be good-humoured and high-spirited, and urged her to buck herself up, suggesting a light-hearted holiday. That was out of the question for Agatha, immersed in clearing out Ashfield and badly missing Carlo's support. For Carlo had been temporarily called back to Scotland where her father was ill.

And while she was locked in the misery of her bereavement, Agatha ignored the womanly-wise advice handed down by her mother. She put her husband's needs second, perhaps subliminally resenting his inadequate support. She was quite unprepared for the bombshell he dropped when he arrived for a short stay at Ashfield looking out of sorts and distracted. She didn't at first believe him when he said he had fallen in love with someone else and wanted a divorce.

But it was perfectly true. Nancy Neele, a secretary 10 years younger than Archie and Agatha, was a friend of friends of the Christies. Without Agatha raising any objection she had become Archie's regular golfing partner. Agatha described herself as too much of a rabbit to accompany him, though, as she had won the club's Ladies' Trophy herself, she may have been excusing her inability to share his obsession.

Although Archie may have dropped tactless hints that Agatha was losing the youthful looks that had originally attracted him, it never occurred to Agatha that loyal and honourable old Archie, devoted to his daughter, could find a more suitable companion for life. It didn't help that, following the respectable middle class convention of the times, the love affair was not cemented with adultery. Whenever Archie and Nancy stayed together it was at the homes of sympathetic friends who protected her reputation with careful chaperonage and separate bedrooms.

AGATHA AT STYLES WITH HER AFRICAN WOODEN ANIMALS.

AGATHA AND ROSALIND.

Since the only ground for divorce at the time was adultery, Archie would have to go through the silly farce of taking a paid "co-respondent" to a Brighton Hotel and ensuring that they were seen compromisingly in the same bed by a chambermaid, even though no actual sex might take place. Agatha contemptuously suggested that Nancy might have the backbone to do her own dirty work. Archie, sounding even more wooden than Captain Hastings, heatedly replied that she was "too straight" for that. Probably Agatha privately wanted Nancy's name dragged through the mud of the courts. Divorce was socially unacceptable. No divorcee had ever been prime minister. The Court of St James's would not accept even the innocent parties to divorce, so Agatha would never be able to present Rosalind at her debut. She refused categorically to divorce Archie, and although supportive Carlo came back to Sunningdale, and Archie's brother Campbell was sympathetic, the couple settled into a few months of intense private misery.

Eleven Days Wonder

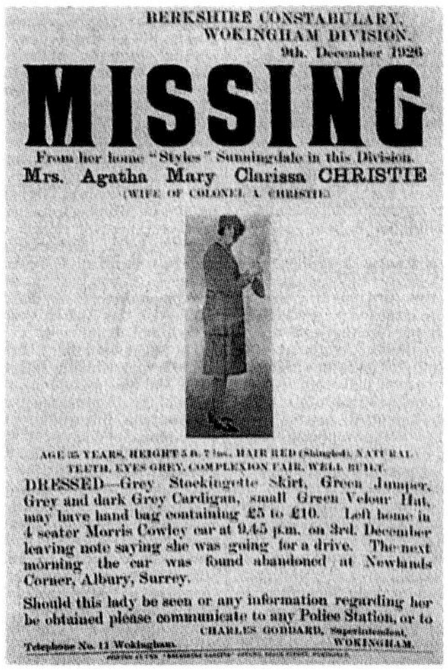
BERKSHIRE CONSTABULARY,
WOKINGHAM DIVISION.
9th. December 1926

MISSING

From her home "Styles" Sunningdale in this Division.
Mrs. Agatha Mary Clarissa CHRISTIE
(WIFE OF COLONEL A. CHRISTIE)

AGE 35 YEARS, HEIGHT 5 ft. 7 ins., HAIR RED (Shingled), NATURAL TEETH, EYES GREY, COMPLEXION FAIR, WELL BUILT.

DRESSED—Grey Stockingette Skirt, Green Jumper, Grey and dark Grey Cardigan, small Green Velour Hat, may have hand bag containing £5 to £10. Left home in 4 seater Morris Cowley car at 9.45 p.m. on 3rd. December leaving note saying she was going for a drive. The next morning the car was found abandoned at Newlands Corner, Albury, Surrey.

Should this lady be seen or any information regarding her be obtained please communicate to any Police Station, or to
CHARLES GODDARD, Superintendent,
Telephone No. 11 Wokingham. WOKINGHAM.

THE POLICE POSTER THAT ACCOMPANIED THE DESPERATE SEARCH FOR THE MISSING WRITER.

On Friday, December 3, there was a row. Agatha knew that Archie was going to stay with friends in Godalming for the weekend and that Nancy would be one of the party. According to her later novel *Unfinished Portrait*, which her second husband described as the best self-portrait to be found in her works, she responded that when Archie came back he wouldn't find her.

Agatha took Rosalind over to visit Archie's mother during the afternoon and laughed hysterically when Mrs Hemsley remarked that she wasn't wearing her wedding ring.

In Styles that evening she wrote a distraught letter for Carlo Fisher, telling her to cancel reservations she had made to stay in Beverley, Yorkshire over the weekend. She wrote a letter reproaching and apparently incriminating Archie which he burned on reading it. She packed an overnight case, and around ten or eleven o' clock, told one of the servants she was going for a drive.

WOMAN WINS OUR £400 PICTURE PUZZLE PRIZE

DAILY SKETCH

INCORPORATING THE DAILY GRAPHIC

No. 5,318. LONDON, WEDNESDAY, DECEMBER 15, 1926. ONE PENNY.

20 Pages
DARK BLUES AGAIN ROUTED AT TWICKENHAM

MRS. AGATHA CHRISTIE FOUND ALIVE

THE DISCOVERY THAT AGATHA CHRISTIE WAS ALIVE MADE THE FRONT-PAGES OF MANY NEWSPAPERS

At 8.00 am the following morning her Morris Cowley was found some 20 miles south of Sunningdale and just five miles out of Godalming. It had gone off the road at Newlands Corner and was stalled with its nose stuck in bushes. Agatha's fur coat and overnight case were still in the car. Of Agatha and her handbag, there was no sign.

Before 8.00 am on Saturday morning, she posted a letter from London to Archie's brother Campbell. He received it on Monday, and the envelope with its postmark survived, though the letter was thrown away before he realized the importance of its message that she was going to a Yorkshire spa. And she bought new overnight things before taking the train to Harrogate. She always carried sufficient cash in a moneybelt for any emergencies, she claimed later.

In Harrogate, "Mrs Teresa Neele of Capetown" checked in to the Hydropathic Hotel (now renamed the Old Swan). For the first few days she covered her face with her hands whenever the servants came into her room. Later she put an ad in *The Times* agony column, asking friends and relatives of Mrs Teresa Neele, late of South Africa, to contact her. During the day she read the papers and did the crosswords. In the evenings she danced and played bridge.

Back in the home counties confusion reigned. There were no signs that the car had gone out of control. It looked as if it had been pushed to where it rested. Police and the press learned about the Christies' marital troubles. Had Agatha committed suicide? Ditches were searched, ponds were dragged. Had her adulterous husband quietly done away with her? It couldn't be asked out loud, but the suspicion was obvious. Archie was understandably exasperated, and suggested that his wife had probably engineered her own disappearance. She had once said she might, he observed.

The press tended to agree. Edgar Wallace, commissioned to "solve" the mystery, theorized that Agatha had absconded to embarrass "somebody" who had hurt her. "Somebody", the world could easily guess, was Colonel Christie, the straying spouse, who now had innuendoes about his straying published all over the nation, and was darkly suspected of murder to boot. Archie's mother made another suggestion: Agatha might have been unable to restart the car after running it off the road, and wandered off with a vague intention of doing away with herself.

And after eleven days it was all over. A chambermaid in the Hydropathic Hotel spotted the likeness between "Mrs Neele" and the missing novelist whose picture was in the papers. She told two dance band players who told the police. Archie was rushed up to Harrogate; identified Agatha; took her away to be examined by a doctor; emerged to tell the press tersely that she was suffering from amnesia and could remember nothing of the last eleven days. And from that moment, the family clammed up and refused to tell the intrusive newshounds anything more about the incident.

The newshounds scoffed at the amnesia story. They, and the police, accepted the revenge-hoax theory, or took it all as a publicity stunt, and condemned Agatha's irresponsibility in setting off an expensive public search. One unproven press report that she wrote to Harrods asking them to send some of her jewelry from store to Harrogate would certainly support their conclusion. If it is true. Harrods have no record of it. Agatha was so bruised by the hostile headlines that she declined publicity for the rest of her life and silently excised all trace of the episode from her memoirs.

And what did happen? Well, she *might* have driven off the road accidentally – the stress she was under would be quite enough to make her driving deteriorate. She *might* have concussed herself or suffered an hysterical amnesiac fugue. On the other hand, she might have faked amnesia to get away from it all, and coincidentally, (either by luck or judgement) punish Archie and bring ghastly publicity to the husband-stealing name of Neele. She had, after all, created Jane Finn, faking amnesia, just four years earlier in *The Secret Adversary*.

CHRISTIE'S MYSTERIOUS DISAPPEARANCE WAS MADE INTO A HOLLYWOOD FILM STARRING VANESSA REDGRAVE AND DUSTIN HOFFMAN.

In 1999 author Jared Cade revealed that Nan Watts's daughter and son-in-law confirmed the punitive hoax story. It had been planned with Nan's co-operation. Nan supplied the cash for new clothes and train fare, obviating that implausible moneybelt. The letter to Campbell should have resulted in early discovery before the press got on to the story. Only Campbell didn't know she had disappeared until after he had lost it. Archie took it all on the chin, rather than have Nancy exposed to press hounding. The weird coincidence that a writer who created a character faking amnesia should have suffered a genuine attack herself disappeared. Distasteful though it seemed to those who wanted Agatha to be a feminist heroine, incapable of petty trickery, the truth was what the newshounds had always believed.

Recovery

A brave public face and a reconciliation were two different matters. Agatha's escapade was roundly condemned. Questions were asked in Parliament about the expenditure of public money in searching for her. Nancy sensibly took herself off abroad and out of the way while Agatha and Archie tried to sort themselves out. Agatha went for "treatment" to a hypnotist – an experience she found more embarrassing than useful. Carlo remained totally loyal and blamed herself for having gone to London on the night of 3 December. James Watts proved solidly reliable and showed Agatha what Carlo had always seen, that there was no possibility of reviving Archie's affection. Campbell Christie encouraged her to turn the 12 Poirot stories she had sold to the *Daily Sketch* into a novel. And the resulting work, *The Big Four*, though "a rotten book" as Agatha knew, kept the money coming in to pay the bills.

These people, and a few other supportive friends, were approved by Agatha as the "OFD" – Order of Faithful Dogs. Those who criticized her or sided with Archie were the Order of Faithless Rats. Rosalind's wire-haired terrier Peter was first among the OFD, and shared with Carlo the dedication to *The Blue Train*, which Agatha had been writing when the catastrophe occurred. While Carlo was away in Scotland, Peter had been her only friend and comforter. (She shrank from letting Madge know what was going on). Beloved dogs played an occasional part in her writing from then on, often attractively described as thinking, feeling characters.

There was really no avoiding divorce now. Agatha divorced Archie in 1927, and he went ahead and married Nancy, with whom he remained happy for the remainder of her life. Agatha stopped taking Holy Communion, fearing embarrassment at the hands of

SANTA CRUZ IN THE CANARIES, WHERE AGATHA VACATIONED TO RECOVER FROM THE STRESS OF 1926.

one of those Anglican clergymen who refused to administer it to divorcees. She retained a bitter little quotation from the Psalms in a writing case, together with Archie's letters, "For it is not an open enemy that hath done me this dishonour … But it was even thou, my companion my guide, and mine own familiar friend."

Long after her life had settled down, the memory of 1926 and 1927 would remain traumatic, an experience she was unwilling to talk about, and which left her with an unusual residue of cynicism. Although her writing showed her to be quite unafraid of her own sexuality, she was nevertheless mistrustful of instantly attractive men. Her heroines are more likely than any other detective writer's to discover that the charming seeming-hero was the real villain all along.

ROSALIND WITH PETER, FIRST OF THE "FAITHFUL DOGS"

Although it took a great effort and a holiday on the Canary Islands with Rosalind and Carlo to complete *The Blue Train*, professional writing was the one area of her life going really well. She had taken on Edmund Cork as her literary agent, the young successor to Hugh Massie, who had been recommended to her by the west country novelist Eden Philpotts when he gave the teenage Agatha Miller some excellent advice on her first apprentice effort at writing a novel. Cork saw her out of the unsatisfactory arrangement with John Lane and into a very good contract with William Collins. The advance of £750 Collins offered for each of her next six novels was almost double what George Orwell reckoned supported a slightly financially strained middle class family at the time. The royalty of 20% rising to 25% was double that offered to unrecognized writers. And since Agatha habitually wrote more than one book a year, she was starting to prosper. She bought a Chelsea mews house in Cresswell Place, and found a good private school for Rosalind. "Caledonia" would turn up as "Meadowbank" in *Cat Among the Pigeons* nearly 30 years later. If Agatha understood its policy aright, it was supposedly "experimental", though this amounted to little more than taking very rich pupils paying high fees to subsidize the brighter and less rich pupils who brought the place academic prestige. It would be characteristic of practical and home-educated Mrs Christie to grasp a commercial experiment more readily than advanced teaching practices.

In 1928 she started what she might have thought of as "serious" writing. Using the pseudonym "Mary Westmacott" – after experimenting again with her grandfather's name "Nathaniel" – she produced *Giant's Bread*, a complicated novel treating a number of topics that mattered to her, including childhood relationships and their carry-over into adult life, love for a childhood home, varying musical ambitions, misplaced love, and most surprisingly for a woman who would never fully overcome her class and period's distaste for Jews, an attempt to consider sympathetically the hostility endured by Jewish arrivants in county society. Five years later the "Mary Westmacott"disguise had worn well enough for her to use it to examine her own marital breakdown under the cover of fiction in *Unfinished Portrait.*

But by the autumn of 1928 she was ready for a holiday and booked a cruise to the West Indies. At the last minute she changed her plans. In dinner conversation with a naval couple who had just returned from Baghdad she learned that the Orient Express led to that fascinating city. And she determined to ride that exciting train and go there.

Ur and the Woolleys

The Orient Express did not let her down, despite being full of bedbugs. Agatha loved train journeys and in old age looked back nostalgically on the age of steam. Poirot and Mr Parker Pyne would both be sent on the Orient Express.

She was less keen on the sympathetic interest other travellers took in her. She didn't really mind being propositioned by gentlemen: she found it flattering as she approached 40. But she did not welcome ladies who wanted to manage her because she was on her own. One particularly intrusive and annoying Englishwoman turned up again on the rickety bus which took Agatha across the desert in the final stage to Baghdad, and then introduced her into the English expatriate circle in the city. Agatha was in search of the exotic, not the kind of society which creates its own Cheltenham wherever it finds itself. This, and the joy she took in the desert, led to another spur-of-the-moment change of plans. She set out for the excavations at the ancient city of Ur.

1920S POSTER FOR THE ORIENT EXPRESS, HIGHLIGHTING LONDON, PARIS, VENICE AND STAMBOUL.

The desert was Agatha's great discovery on this journey. She exulted in its solitude and tangible silence. She now understood fully why Jesus and John the Baptist had gone to the wilderness for spiritual refreshment. Her late "Mary Westmacott" novels show that she believed that being in the desert without the distraction of reading matter was a way to the most intense self-exploration, and could lead to almost mystical changes of personality.

Ur was in the news. It was of interest to archaeologists because it was the early capital of Sumerian civilization, the forerunner of the great Babylonian and Assyrian empires. The Sumerians had invented cuneiform writing, impressing little golf-tee-shaped wedges in wet clay to form a lasting script. And to the delight of Victorian scholars, the translation of cuneiform records proved that the biblical books of Kings and Chronicles gave an accurate historical picture of the great empires.

Leonard Woolley, the excavator of Ur, learned his archaeology with Lawrence of Arabia, digging up crusader castles in the Middle East. He also learned from Lawrence the value of publicity. Ur was a site attracting the attention of Christendom and Jewry, since everyone knew that the Patriarch Abraham hailed from Ur of the Chaldees before God promised him and his descendants

EXCAVATIONS AT UR.

the land flowing with milk and honey which turned out to be Palestine. Woolley went further, by announcing that he had found traces of a great flood which was presumably that recorded in the recently translated Sumerian *Epic of Gilgamesh*, and that celebrated in the Bible as Noah's flood. He was wrong, actually. The flood he had found preceded Noah's by about 1000 years. But his mistake added to the popular interest in his work.

So did his discovery of treasure. Since the opening of Tutankhamun's tomb, the press and public hoped for more dramatic discoveries of exotic hoards of golden artefacts. Woolley found precious objects buried in the 2000 grave sites around Ur. He also introduced the literate world to the ziggurat, the curious step-sided pyramid-shaped building on which later generations of Babylonians modelled their world-famous hanging gardens.

Agatha's interest in archaeology had emerged in South Africa, where she was fascinated by the discovery of skulls and crude Bushman implements in the veldt. Mesopotamian archaeology was even more wonderful. She did not know that archaeologists didn't really welcome curious sightseers at their digs. But she was lucky. Woolley's party was dominated by his wife Katharine, a strikingly good-looking woman who insisted on being the centre of attention. She used her sex appeal to manipulate men, and, like many women of her kind, did not like having other women around to challenge her role as Queen Bee. But she liked knowing celebrities. And the author of *Roger Ackroyd* had written a book she knew and enjoyed. Agatha was also quiet, unflamboyant and uncompetitive. Katharine Woolley condescended to make her welcome and urged her to extend her stay. Agatha had to get home for Rosalind's Christmas holidays, but she accepted an invitation to revisit the dig the following year. It would prove a fateful visit.

On her way back to England she met a Colonel Dwyer in Baghdad who had been in the King's African Rifles where he knew Monty as "Puffing Billy Miller". Since Monty was still a burden on his sisters, who had sent him to Marseilles for the milder climate, Agatha was pleased to learn that her dashing but demanding elder brother had impressed his comrades as utterly fearless, for all his eccentricities. Monty died suddenly of a stroke the following year. Agatha's account in her *Autobiography* suggests that the colonel fell a little bit in love with her, and she gave serious thought to going on expeditions with this adventurous lonely man, separated from a stay-at-home wife and children.

Another Baghdad acquaintance had pointed out to her that she was sure to have a lover: her real choice lay between one and several. She realized with her customary frankness that he was quite right, as she feared repeating the commitment of marriage, though she felt that promiscuity would not really suit her.

LEONARD WOOLLEY.

Max Mallowan

The year 1929 was a busy one for Agatha. She wrote her first play, *Black Coffee*, having been mildly dissatisfied with Michael Morton's dramatization of *Roger Ackroyd* as *Alibi* the previous year. She created new characters who would recur, Mr Harley Quin and Miss Jane Marple. She lent Cresswell Place to the Woolleys in the spring and definitely arranged to go out to Ur again in the summer and travel back with them via the Mediterranean and Delphi.

LANCING COLLEGE, MAX MALLOWAN'S PUBLIC SCHOOL.

On this second visit to Ur she fully appreciated Colonel Dwyer's warning that, for all her charm, Katharine Woolley was unpredictable, demanding and – much as Agatha felt she liked her – a pain in the neck. The young assistants at the dig fluttered round the domineering director's wife like courtiers, a role which, as George Orwell pointed out, English public school men learn young under prep school headmaster's wives, who take up and drop favourites as capriciously as Elizabeth I.

Among the young men was the director's Assistant, Max Mallowan, who had not been at Ur the previous season. Fourteen years younger than Agatha, Max had been lucky to get the post with Woolley on coming down from Oxford, where he had taken an abysmal fourth-class degree. In today's meritocratic age, this would have blocked any hope of a learned career. But he had been to a sufficiently "pukka" school (Evelyn Waugh's and Tom Driberg's Lancing), and he proved a good linguist, a meticulous observer and a hard worker, well suited to practical archaeology. He was also, Agatha observed, one of the most obliging people at the dig, often capable of handling Katharine Woolley when others could not, and outstandingly good at dealing with the native labourers. It seemed, however, that Katharine was imposing on him when, at the end of the season, she declared that Max was to take Agatha on a tour of major Mesopotamian archaeological sites before handing her over to the Woolleys for their planned trip to Delphi. Max, however, accepted the proposal equably, saying he welcomed the chance to visit other people's interesting digs.

The journey through the desert made Max and Agatha good friends. Particularly memorable was their discovery of a beautiful blue lake and Agatha's sportingly agreeing to find sufficiently stout underwear for them to enjoy a swim together. On their emergence, their car proved to be stuck in the sand. Max and the driver toiled and sweated with mats and stones to try and move it. Agatha peacefully lay in the vehicle's shade and went to sleep. Her cheerful and uncomplaining attitude to this misadventure made a great impression on Max.

He made a great impression on her when they joined the Woolleys in Athens, and Agatha found a pile of telegrams from Madge telling her that Rosalind had pneumonia, a very serious illness in those days before antibiotics. The Delphi plan had to be dropped. Agatha had to get a place on the Orient Express and head for home at once. Max quietly changed his plans and accompanied her. When they left the train to buy oranges in Milan, and it steamed away before they could rejoin it, he pooled his money with hers to hire a fast car and chase it to the next stop. The car was so expensive that Agatha had to borrow money from Max's mother in Paris to complete her journey.

Fortunately Rosalind was on the mend by the time she reached home. After their adventures, Max was, Agatha felt, one of her dearest friends, and he was invited to Ashfield for a holiday of picnics and walks in the misty rain on Dartmoor. And one night he astonished Agatha by coming to her room to return a book, and telling her he wanted to marry her. She objected that the age difference was too great. He had thought of that. She objected that he was a Catholic and she was Anglican. He had thought of that. She objected for two hours against his gentle persistence, before she realized that the only objection that never occurred to her was the idea that she didn't want to marry him. For, although she had never thought of it before, she knew that she did.

Punkie objected strongly on grounds of age. And the age difference worried Agatha all over again when she found that Max had been up at New College with her nephew Jack. But James Watts was mild in his objections. Carlo backed Agatha up, though more out of loyalty than conviction, Agatha believed. Katharine Woolley gave the engagement her lofty blessing, with the proviso that Max would have to wait two years, as things should not be too easy for him. And Rosalind, having ensured that Agatha knew she would have to share her bed with a husband if she married, approved Max more than any of the other suitors she had watched with precocious intelligence.

MAX AND AGATHA IN WINTERBROOK, THE HOUSE SHE BROUGHT FOR HIM IN WALLINGFORD.

The Catholic problem evanesced when Max, an Oxford convert, discovered that his church would refuse to recognize his marriage to a divorcee. Outraged by matrimonial laws devised by celibates, Max left the church. Katharine Woolley's impertinence was ignored. The couple were married quietly in Edinburgh to avoid any possible publicity, after Agatha had spent three happy weeks resident in Skye having the banns published where no reporter would hear them. She had made one of the best decisions of her life.

Success and Houses

AGATHA AND MAX AT WINTERBROOK HOUSE, 1944.

Their honeymoon took them to Venice, Yugoslavia and Greece. Their interests differed predictably. Agatha loved the Lido and came to feel she had seen enough churches; Max swam dutifully wherever they could, and enjoyed the historical remains. Agatha felt she had been carried too far up an exhausting mule track and was surely too old for her husband, until she enjoyed the exquisite monuments he knew awaited them.

Katharine Woolley no longer welcomed Agatha at Ur. There was no place for married women in her court, and Leonard, always under his wife's thumb, suggested that Agatha ought not even to travel as far as Baghdad with Max. The Mallowans were furious, but having already decided that they would go their separate ways after Greece, did not cut off their noses to spite their faces. But when Agatha came down with serious food poisoning after over-indulging in seafood, it was outrageous that the Woolleys insisted Max must go ahead to the excavations without seeing her fit to travel. And then they arrived a month late themselves! Max took his revenge by building Katharine's bathroom so small that it had to be torn down and replaced when she came. And with conscious naughtiness and Max's encouragement, Agatha portrayed the Ur archaeologists in *Murder in Mesopotamia* with Katharine as an insufferable excavation director's wife who is quite satisfactorily murdered.

As the season progressed, Max took up an offer to go to Nineveh with a different party the following year. And subsequently he headed his own digs, once in Iraq and thereafter, as the political situation became more tense, in Syria. Agatha then joined his parties as a seriously contributing member. She tried unsuccessfully to draw the important finds. She took photography lessons after encouraging Rosalind to abandon ambitions of being a photographic model and work behind the lens instead. Her artistic impressions of light and shade were not the images Max wanted to use to record the precise dimensions of his discoveries. But she sorted and listed sherds, and made her own contribution to field archaeology by developing the use of orange sticks and face cream to clean them.

And while in the field, Agatha wrote. Her writing entered its greatest period as her marriage to Max Mallowan bloomed. The short stories in the collection *The Listerdale Mystery* are not her finest work. But they include a high proportion of happy romantic tales, showing how Mrs Christie's wounds were healing on Mrs Mallowan. Superb whodunnits of the 1930s included *The Sittaford Mystery, Lord Edgware Dies, The ABC Murders, Death on the Nile, Murder on the Orient Express* and *And Then There Were None.*

THE "COLLINS CRIME CLUB" EDITION OF *THE A.B.C. MURDERS.*

Conan Doyle died in 1930. Edgar Wallace followed two years later. Ronald Knox gave up crime fiction to translate the Bible. Agatha Christie's position was now well to the forefront of crime writers. But not yet, in the eyes of the intelligentsia, in the topmost position. When her old publisher John Lane's nephew Allen revolutionized the trade by starting the Penguin library in 1935, Agatha Christie's *Murder on the Links* was number six of the first 10 sixpenny paperbacks that launched the series. But number five was *The Unpleasantness at the Bellona Club.* Dorothy L. Sayers had the edge on Mrs Christie in commanding intellectual respect, and it was the rather bossy Dorothy Sayers who organized Agatha into joining teams of detective writers to prepare jointly written whodunnit serials for radio. After the third Agatha refused any more. It was an unprofitable use of her time to write these short pieces.

And her time was now very profitable. This was her "prosperous" period when American advances and royalties came in without being taxed. Rosalind went from Caledonia to Benenden, and thence to finishing schools in Switzerland and Paris before making a full debut in the London season. Agatha bought property. She let Cresswell Place and bought a larger house in Sheffield Terrace, Kensington. Here, for the only time in her life, she had the Virginia Woolf ideal, "a room of her own", with armchair, sofa, large writing table and chair, and a Steinway grand piano. Usually, like Jane Austen, she was capable of writing in rooms where other people came and went and talked. She bought Winterbrook House, a Queen Anne house in Wallingford, as a country weekend place that was less difficult to reach than Torquay. She always regarded this pleasant place beside the Thames as Max's house, since it was easily accessible to his beloved Oxford.

And, in 1938, when it became clear that Tor suburb had expanded all over the lanes behind Ashfield, and the great Victorian villas had all been cut up into flats or taken over as nursing homes, she finally sold Ashfield and bought Greenway, a splendid Queen Anne house near Dartmouth overlooking the river Dart. She had it restored and redecorated to her taste with a big shelf by her bath to hold the apples she, like her creation Mrs Oliver, loved to eat while bathing. This beautiful property, with acres of land running down to the river and its own little boathouse featured in three of her novels *Five Little Pigs, Towards Zero, Dead Man's Folly.* Hitler's war broke into an idyllic life Agatha had earned and deserved.

GREENWAY, AGATHA'S DEVONSHIRE HOME OVERLOOKING THE DART.

World War Two

PETER USTINOV AS POIROT, WITH MAGGIE SMITH AS A RARE WOMAN WHO WON HIS ADMIRATION IN THE MOVIE VERSION OF *EVIL UNDER THE SUN.*

EVIL UNDER THE SUN: AN IMPROVED AND EXPANDED VERSION OF "TRIANGLE AT RHODES".

The prospect of war affected Max's work. He could not risk digging in the Middle East in 1939 and turned down an invitation to an archaeological convention in Berlin in August. When war came he tried desperately to get into some form of active service or war work, hampered by the fact that he was too old and untrained for recruitment into the armed forces, and although he was born in England and seemed the epitome of the English public school and Oxbridge academic, he had, as a matter of fact, hardly any English blood at all, being Hungarian on his father's side and French on his mother's.

After a typically unsatisfactory period drilling with no rifles in the Torquay Home Guard, he managed to get a job organizing humanitarian aid to earthquake victims in Turkey, and then a commission in the RAF Volunteer Reserve and work in the Air Ministry. In 1941 he was promoted to Squadron Leader and posted to Cairo where he found his brother Cecil running the British Council. Max spent the remainder of the war in the Middle East carrying out a variety of administrative and magisterial duties.

War had a curious effect on the books Agatha published in the early 1940s. *Evil Under the Sun* was an effective expansion of a Poirot short story, translating its locale from Rhodes to Burgh Island off the Devon coast.

It betrayed its naive pre-war composition by linking Mussolini with Princess Elizabeth as characters who are "too risky" to use in a game of "Who would you rather be?". *One, Two, Buckle My Shoe* also showed Agatha preoccupied with the problem of dictators. In this book she expounds her belief that mega-rich British financiers and the dullness of their support for the democratic establishment are the best answer to Hitler and Mussolini. There is no evidence that a war is going on, which may be why the American publishers insisted on its being retitled *The Patriotic Murders*, to justify the grumbling undertow of political reference. *N or M*, by contrast, is a deliberately patriotic wartime thriller which Agatha and Max felt – more strongly than we can today – was powerfully anti-Nazi. America thought so too during the election in which F.D. Roosevelt was returned with an isolationist congress, and Dodd, Mead did not publish the book until late in 1941. *The Body in the Library*, on the other hand, is an excellent Miss Marple mystery which seems to take place in peacetime until the very last minute when the author needs to rehabilitate a louche and trendy suspect. At this point it is revealed that he was secretly married to the woman everyone in St Mary Mead took to be his mistress, and that he was seriously injured while bravely carrying out Anti Air-Raid Protection work, and so is not a slacker or a conchie – the lowest forms of political life for Agatha at the time.

After this, Agatha seems to have felt that including the war dated her novels too precisely and might hinder ongoing sales. *The Moving Finger* is told from the point of view of a pilot recuperating from a crash. Since there is apparently nothing unusual about such a convalescence, he seems extraordinarily likely to have been injured in the Battle of Britain. But this probability is never mentioned, and there is no sign of a war going on. *Timelessness* was essential in *Curtain* and *Sleeping Murder*, respectively Poirot's and Miss Marple's "last cases", written for publication after Agatha's death. And in *Towards Zero* the story is deliberately timeless. There are pointers however. The whole family listens daily to the evening news on the wireless, a habit which developed during the war. And although they don't dress for dinner in the summer, they apparently do in the winter, a domestic habit which did not survive the war.

After Max left for the Turkish relief organization in London, Greenway was invaded by tenants and evacuees before being requisitioned as headquarters for the US Naval force stationed at Dartmouth. Agatha went to join Max in London, but could not use either of her own houses. Cresswell Place was let and Sheffield Terrace was unsafe after the bombing. They had to stay in a Bauhaus flat in Hampstead found for them by Max's archaeological colleague, Stephen Glanville. Agatha was lonely and missed Max badly when he was posted to Cairo. They wrote regular loving letters keeping each other informed about everything they were doing. Carlo had taken up war work in a factory. Rosalind, after filling in forms to join the WAAFs or the ATS, married Herbert Prichard, an officer of the Royal Welsh Fusiliers from a good county family on the Welsh border. When their son Mathew was born in 1942, Agatha came to help Rosalind as often as she could, causing Mathew's nurse to tell her parents that Agatha Christie, writer of a play they had so much enjoyed, was "our cook". Agatha herself felt that she was unable to give Rosalind the emotional support she needed when Herbert was killed in 1944.

***THE BODY IN THE LIBRARY*: A MISS MARPLE MYSTERY SET IN WORLD WAR TWO.**

Agatha's own war work was largely a return to dispensing at University College Hospital. Shortly before Mathew was born she broke it off for three days, pleading an imaginary indisposition. In fact, she wrote the Mary Westmacott novel *Absent in the Spring*, completing it in the three days and giving herself an aching back. This compulsive need to write a serious book, with her uncharacteristic desertion of duty to do so, is one of the clearest signs we have that Agatha Christie was, by temperament, a creative artist and not a commercial hack.

Queen of Crime

Max's return six months after the war ended was a happy reunion. Agatha was a little concerned that she had grown fat. She needn't have worried. So had Max, and he couldn't have cared less about her size.

They took a small flat in Chelsea with Cresswell Place let. And when Greenway returned to them, they set to work restoring it to its former glory. An officer had painted a frieze around the living room showing all the places his unit had travelled, ending with a view of Greenway and the Dart. This delighted Agatha, who retained it. She did not, however, require the fifteen lavatories installed beside the kitchen, and it took a good deal of correspondence to persuade the authorities to remove them.

AGATHA IN FRONT OF THE FRIEZE THAT SO DELIGHTED HER AT GREENWAY HOUSE AFTER THE WAR.

Another difficult correspondence with authority threatened her with bankruptcy. Before the war the American Internal Revenue Service had made a sudden huge demand on Agatha for income tax. This was disputed and negotiated on her behalf by her American agent and a tax lawyer. But after the outbreak of war, the US authorities froze all her advances and royalties until the negotiations were complete and a settlement was reached. This might not have mattered, had not the British Income Tax suddenly insisted on claiming their proportion of the American earnings that had not been paid. The demand for money she hadn't got was so excessive that Agatha Christie, while earning extremely well, was in constant difficulties. She had to consider selling Greenway. She struggled on until at last an agreement was reached with the American tax men, and her taxed earnings were released to her. By that time British income tax had risen to the point where the more she worked, the less she was rewarded. She grumbled in good company, but after 1950 never again saw her actual solvency threatened by exorbitant taxes. She did realize that it had become financially necessary to reduce her prolific output to about one book a year. In 1948 she was under such stress that she wrote nothing for 12 months, a unique break in her output. Thereafter occasional outbreaks of psoriasis showed how deeply she had been affected.

Although Agatha's American earnings were rising, her agents in the USA were not sure how long this would continue. Dorothy Sayers had left the field, complaining mildly that her detective fiction was not properly appreciated, and trying to establish a more serious intellectual reputation as a religious playwright and translator of medieval classics. It seemed that the 1930s fad for detective puzzles solved by eccentric private detectives or brilliant amateurs was giving way to greater realism. Reviewers preferred police heroes like Simenon's Maigret or Ngaio Marsh's Alleyne. Alternatively, the hard-boiled Californian school of Dashiell Hammett and Raymond Chandler sent tight-lipped private eyes who were not themselves mean down the mean streets around Malibu and Muscle Beach. They were both more realistic and more dryly witty than Hercule Poirot. Agatha detested the hard-boiled form, and Raymond Chandler returned the compliment.

POSTWAR NOVELS: AGATHA'S FAVOURITE WHODUNNIT AND A PREPOSTEROUS THRILLER.

ously, and naming her the Queen of Crime. One by one her women rivals, Dorothy Sayers, Ngaio Marsh and Margery Allingham, were given the same treatment. In each case, however, it was recalled that Agatha Christie had been first on the throne of crime fiction.

Her thrillers were almost equally marketable, though even her publishers were beginning to raise eyebrows at them. Collins' reader thought that *They Came to Baghdad* must have been intended as a joke. Since Agatha had not yet committed herself to the Cold War with Soviet agents as the automatic "bad guys", she invented a violent revolutionary conspiracy of the Centre, aiming to foment a war in which capitalists and communists would destroy each other and open the way for a dictatorship of moderation. This bizarre notion makes the book feel as incongruous as one of those Peter Van Greenaway thrillers in which *Rambo*-esque violence is used to enforce the softest of left ideals. *They Came to Baghdad*, though, leaves one with an uneasy feeling that Roehm, Strasser and some other victims of Hitler's purge of the brownshirts might have approved the concept. Agatha had not been out of date when she wrote silly thrillers in the age of Sapper and Dornford Yates. She was starting to feel distinctly geriatric, however, in the company of ideologically advanced Eric Ambler or the genuinely apolitical Hammond Innes.

RUPERT DAVIES (LEFT) AND GEORGES SIMENON, THE INTERPRETER AND CREATOR OF THE REALISTIC INSPECTOR MAIGRET.

This, perhaps, blinded the serious critics to her continuing merits. In postwar books like *Mrs McGinty's Dead, They Do It With Mirrors* and her personal favourite, *The Crooked House*, she continued to devise the best and most laterally-thought-out puzzles on the market in settings which faithfully reflected changing social surfaces with an underlying nostalgia for traditional (Edwardian) Britain, like the drawings of the cartoonist Giles.

In the end, her sales did not fall away. The market for her work and that of John Dickson Carr (Carter Dickson), Margery Allingham, Anthony Berkeley and the other soft-centred crime writers stayed solid. The instantly identifiable greenbacked Penguin Crime series paid her the compliment of reissuing 10 of her books simultane-

The Road TO THE Mousetrap

Agatha was an avid and omnivorous theatregoer, enjoying Chekhov or the opera as much as the latest comedy or musical. She wrote her own first play, *Black Coffee*, because she was dissatisfied with Michael Morton's dramatization of *Roger Ackroyd.* Francis L. "Larry" Sullivan realized Poirot to her satisfaction and became a close friend, though the play is not very interesting. Agatha had not yet grasped that the essence of stage thrillers is the surprise of what happens next, not the slow unravelling of a puzzle. She was not alone in mishandling the form. Brian Delane's *Who Killed the Count?,* a comedy thriller of 1938 which imitated the central idea of *Murder on the Orient Express*, has a tedious second act in which a police inspector laboriously interviews three suspects.

MARGARET LOCKWOOD.

Apart from the lavish historical play *Akhnaton,* which was too expensive to mount, Agatha did not return to writing for the theatre until the war. Other dramatists made successful stage versions of some of her novels – notably Arnold Ridley, whose huge success with *The Ghost Train* enabled him to live comfortably on the royalties from amateur productions and write or act in whatever pleased him, until in the 1970s his face became nationally familiar as the aged and weak-bladdered Private Godfrey in *Dad's Army.*

But when Agatha heard that *And Then There Were None* was about to be adapted by somebody else, she realized that she wanted to do the job herself. She saw exactly how to alter the ending to give a satisfying conclusion,without losing any of the suspense. And she was moved later when she learned that a translation of the play somehow reached Buchenwald, where survivors told her that mounting a production had given them a tremendous relief from the horrors around.

In 1946 the BBC discovered that Queen Mary was an admirer of Agatha Christie and would like a radio play by her as an 80th birthday celebration. Agatha accepted the commission, stipulating that her fee go to the Southport Infirmary Children's Toys Fund. She adapted her short story *Three Blind Mice* into a 20-minute suspenser, and proved herself an outstanding writer for radio. The three descending notes repeated on the piano easily became a sinister motif. Her two later radio plays, *Personal Call* and *Butter in a Lordly Dish* made excellent use, respectively, of railway station sound effects and the magnificently sinister lines from the Song of Deborah (Judges V, 24-30) describing Jael's assassination of Sisera with a tent peg through the head.

By 1950 she had enjoyed success with several more stage adaptations, notably her own version of *The Hollow*, in which the character and variety actress Jeanne de Casalis ("Mrs Feather") extracted every last ounce of comedy from her eccentric leading role. Agatha was good at tailoring parts to individuals. *The Spider's Web* was deliberately created as a vehicle for Margaret Lockwood. The heroine of *The Lady Vanishes* and *The Wicked Lady* was perfectly suited to the sort of lively good-sport female lead Agatha had created earlier in "Bundle" Brent. And *The Spider's Web* was a perfect frame for the mature

THE MOUSETRAP: STILL THE WORLD'S LONGEST RUNNING PLAY.

Lockwood charm, containing also two delightful old buffer roles for Wilfred Hyde White and Felix Aylmer, and a fine part for Margaret Lockwood's 14-year-old daughter.

In 1951 Agatha started expanding *Three Blind Mice* into a three-act play. Its title had to be changed as there was already a play of that name. Rosalind's second husband, Anthony Hicks, suggested *The Mousetrap*, which Agatha found very satisfying, although it doesn't have any apparent relevance to the play. The vehicle was for Richard Attenborough and Sheila Sims. Like *The Spider's Web* and the subsequent play *Witness for the Prosecution* (which joined them to give Agatha three plays running at once in the West End) it uses a quick clean murder as an exciting curtain, proof that Agatha had now mastered the difference between plays and whodunnit novels, in which she almost invariably kept the actual killing out of sight. *The Mousetrap*'s amazing longevity – it will be 50 in 2002, and has been the world's longest-running play for decades – is really the result of its producer Peter Saunders' successful publicity stunts. When audiences started flagging, he noisily celebrated its 1000th performance; then gave it an annual birthday party and invited the press, until it had become an institution. After six years it had become the longest-running British play ever, and attracted coach parties simply for that reason. Today, when musicals and farces may run for decades, *The Mousetrap*'s headstart pulls in international tourist audiences to see what will probably remain the world's longest run ever. There is really no other reason to watch a not very distinguished play from a poor period.

Witness for the Prosecution is a better example of the genre, and Agatha much preferred her serious play *Victim,* although it bombed with terrible notices. It contains a murder, but not a mystery. The wise perception that idealists can be very dangerous was not really suited to a writer with Agatha's unsophisticated political outlook. But essentially, as she seems to have perceived, neither her reputation nor her experience was likely to succeed in proffering a study of murder as anything but a puzzle or a chiller.

AGATHA AT A REHEARSAL FOR *WITNESS FOR THE PROSECUTION.*

Nimrud

In 1947 Max was appointed Professor of Western Asiatic Archaeology at London University's Institute of Archaeology. Now he could return to regular summer excavations. His digs after Nineveh had mostly been into Syrian Tells – the hillocks that one of his assistants called "bumps" in the Middle Eastern landscape, indicating the presence of buried remains. With the war over and the shifting alliances of Middle Eastern states no longer threatening, it was possible to return to his first love, Sumerian remains in Iraq.

After discussions with the authorities in Baghdad, it was agreed that he should excavate the city of Nimrud, the ancient Sumerian military capital. From 1948 to 1960 this project dominated his professional life, and Agatha gave much of her time over to being "the Director's wife" and an essential member of the team that worked through the annual January to March digging season. Austin Henry Layard, the Victorian diplomat who dug up many of the Assyrian remains that now grace the British Museum, had shoved a spade into Nimrud and found some fine ivory carvings. But he had never excavated it fully. Stonework and bits of statuary sticking out of the ground showed the extent of the site. Max set himself the task of mapping the city and making plans of the forts and palaces, as well as recovering artefacts.

It was unquestionably an important site, one of the three great cities of ancient Assyria. Agatha had absorbed an archaeologist's perspective, and realized that uncovering and recording the details of Nimrud was a piece of work on a par with the excavation of Knossos or Ur, or the opening of Tutankhamun's tomb. But there would not be treasures on the Pharaonic scale, and Nimrud was

KING FEISAL OF IRAQ (FRONT); STANDING BEHIND (SECOND RIGHT) IS T.E. LAWRENCE.

not a familiar name from the Bible or Greek mythology. So while Max's huge investment of time and skill was recognized by his peers, he never enjoyed the general public prestige that was granted Sir Arthur Evans and Sir Leonard Woolley and Howard Carter.

Agatha was the expedition's photographer. She bought a new camera and developed her films in the expedition's dining room in the evenings. Unfortunately, Max and his assistants went to the living room above it after dinner, and if they walked around, flakes of mud would fall from the ceiling into the developing baths.

Agatha also cleaned and catalogued many of the finds. She used Immoxa cleansing milk to remove soil, and damp towels for slowly drying out sodden objects brought up from wells after centuries of immersion. She kept notes. And she amused the team with light verses, laughing at herself and them.

She also wrote and corrected proofs at Nimrud. The Iraqi authorities were unhappy about the parcels of books and printed papers she received. Since they came sealed at both ends, it was feared they might contain bombs. Or communist propaganda. King Feisal and his Prime Minister, Nuri-es-Said, had both been threatened with assassination. And although the monarchy had been established by the British in the 1920s in partial fulfilment of TE Lawrence's promises to the Hashemite dynasty, Agatha Christie's quietly four-square British imperialism was not recognized by suspicious customs officials with poor English. When they opened a package and found proofs of *A Pocket Full of Rye*, they concluded that this was part of a sinister conspiracy to destabilize the country's agriculture.

A few years into the decade of work at Nimrud, Agatha had a separate room built for herself where she could write. This was the place labelled "Beit Agatha" (Agatha's house) in cuneiform, and there she started work on her *Autobiography*, a beautifully written memoir of her childhood and young womanhood which gives us one of the best accounts we have of pre-1914 leisure class life. It is fine social history simply because the Millers were undistinguished. We are not distracted by an interest in the famous people or important incidents which inevitably seize our attention in lives of statesmen or major artists. Some of the unassuming charm apparent in Agatha's letters to Max comes through, and this unhurried work, not to be published until after her death, was hailed when it appeared as possibly the best thing she had written.

In 1960 the digging came to an end. Feisal had been overthrown and killed two years earlier. It was time for Max to devote another 10 years to meticulously writing up his discoveries. The splendid artefacts he had discovered were divided between Iraq and Britain. Mementos of the great work were left in the local British School of Archaeology, including Agatha's straw hat. Max's will included provision for an annual dinner at the British School in Iraq which should always have at least one member of the Mallowan, Miller or Prichard family in attendance.

Max Mallowan might not be a household name. He was never a television personality, like his colleague Sir Mortimer Wheeler (slipped into Agatha's *They Came to Baghdad* as Sir Rupert Crofton Lee). But his magnum opus gave him a well-deserved reputation among scholars, and like his wife, he ended his life with full public honours.

ABOVE: AGATHA AND PRINCE ABDULLAH INSPECTING IVORIES EXCAVATED AT NIMRUD. *OPPOSITE*: AGATHA AT NIMRUD; MAX WORKING IN THE FOREGROUND.

"Honour, Love, Obedience..."

A PICNIC ON DARTMOOR: ROSALIND AND MATHEW ARE ON THE LEFT, AGATHA THE RIGHT.

"Honour, love, obedience, troops of friends", Macbeth's summary of the perfect old age has never been bettered. Agatha Christie deservedly enjoyed them all.

Honours came first from publishers. The American Pocket Books Library awarded her a Golden Gertie in 1948, a statuette of their kangaroo logo in recognition of the sale of a million of her books. In 1951 *Ellery Queen's Mystery Magazine* polled its readers for the top 10 active mystery writers. They ruled out Dorothy L. Sayers as no longer writing crime fiction, though their real anxiety was to eliminate the ex-communist Dashiell Hammett, victimized by McCarthyism. Naturally Agatha Christie came high up the list.

In 1956 she was awarded a CBE in the New Year honours list. The times had changed since a divorcee could not be recognized by the Court of St James's, meaning that friends had had to present Rosalind at her debut. Now Agatha Christie was known as one of the royal family's favourite authors. The Queen had even gone to a special performance of *The Mousetrap* in Windsor. Agatha chortled over the CBE as "one up for the lowbrows", a title she was inclined to bestow on herself when in the company of archaeologists who read and enjoyed Greek and Latin literature in the original. But although her celebrity had meant that some visitors to Nimrud were felt to have been looking for the creator of Hercule Poirot rather than the remains of a great city, she was never prepared to let Max's genuine standing be submerged in her popular fame. When the University of Pennsylvania awarded him a gold medal that year, she insisted that she was accompanying him as Mrs Mallowan and did not want any fuss about Agatha Christie.

In 1960 Max caught up with his wife and was awarded a CBE before taking Agatha on a trip to Persia, India and Ceylon where he opened new schools and institutes for British archaeologists. This trip demonstrated to Agatha (rather to her surprise) that she had many fans in Pakistan. Indeed, the following year UNESCO reported that she was the most widely read English author in the world, outstripping her nearest rival, Graham Greene, by almost doubling his sales. She had been translated into more languages than Shakespeare. None of this turned Agatha's head. She was well aware that over the passage of time Shakespeare would again overtake her, and explicitly listed Greene with Muriel Spark and Elizabeth Bowen, writers whose superior work she would have emulated if she could.

In 1962 Max was elected a Fellow of All Souls College, Oxford, an immensely prestigious non-teaching position

AGATHA WITH HER GRANDSON, MATHEW PRICHARD.

which allowed him to concentrate on writing up the Nimrud excavations. Agatha now listed some heavyweight academics among the friends who read and evaluated her work. John Sparrow, warden of All Souls, and the Byzantine historian Sir Stephen Runciman both congratulated her on *Endless Night.*

In 1967 Max moved ahead of his wife with a knighthood. Agatha became Lady Mallowan. Four years later she received her own personal title and ended her life as Dame Agatha Christie, DBE.

Love came from Max, the supportive love which so completely healed the wounds of passion that she was able to write a kindly sympathetic note to Archie Christie in 1958 when Nancy died. Madge visited less frequently as arthritis bedevilled her old age in the 1940s. Until her death in 1951, her undoubted affection for Agatha was probably tinged with an elder sister's protectiveness. Rosalind offered the clear-eyed love that children of divorcees can often bring to both parents. She was happy in her marriage to Anthony Hicks, whose excellent and wide-ranging tastes and knowledge of Sanskrit made him a perfect younger companion for Max. Agatha sometimes wished her husband and son-in-law were less enthusiastic in discussing wines, which didn't interest her.

Her grandson gave her great pleasure. She was quietly amused and contented that Mathew had done so well by her gift to him of the royalties from *The Mousetrap.* (The less profitable *Curtain* and *Sleeping Murder* had long been bequeathed to Max and Rosalind). Some of the happiest pictures of Agatha show the fat old lady with thick ankles surrounded by her family, picnicking on Dartmoor, or taking Mathew out from school.

Obedience and troops of friends went together. Apart from holding very strong views about the wrappers of her books, and insisting on some artistic changes, Agatha had never been one to order others about. Yet as she became both her agents' and her publishers' best earner, her wishes were quickly acceded to. And her personality was such that business associates easily became friends. Billy Collins sent her parcels of books when they were difficult to find in Devon. Allen Lane sent a Stilton cheese every year for the delectation of the diggers at Nimrud. Harold Ober, her New York agent, went in search of a camera with flash attachment for her. Edmund Corke, her London agent, sent her flowers for anniversaries, got her tickets for the Coronation, protected her from his perception that *Passenger to Frankfurt* was terrible rubbish. All these men shielded her from hostile criticism. And when Agatha started to decline in 1971, she was indeed supported by honour, love, obedience, troops of friends.

Reputation

ROBERT GRAVES.

In the late 1960s Dame Helen Gardner, at that time a dominating figure in the Oxford Faculty of English, made a disparaging remark to me about a colleague who read Agatha Christie. At that time, nobody with any pretensions to critical ability would have questioned that a Fellow of St Hilda's College was passing her time contemptibly in such bland entertainment. When Brigid Brophy complained that a new Agatha Christie was not properly clued so that it could be fairly solved, the surprise was that a journalist with intellectual credentials still took any interest in the outdated game of working out whodunnit. Frankly, reading Agatha Christie was a form of intellectual slumming. She wasn't violently distasteful like Mickey Spillane. But she was flat and shallow. Her world view was dully conventional. Her characters were soap opera stereotypes. Her prose was nerveless and unarresting.

As for her plays, they were cheap entertainment suitable for amateur theatricals or Women's Institute coach parties. Their heyday came in the theatrical doldrums after Shaw, when the verse drama of T.S. Eliot and Christopher Fry failed to please; Terence Rattigan's potential was firmly reined in to a J.B. Priestley level, lest his mother or the legendary matinee-goer "Aunt Edna" noticed his homosexuality; drab well-made plays by N.F. Simpson failed to compete with the American realism of Tennessee Williams and William Inge. The Royal Court Theatre and *Waiting for Godot* had yet to revitalize the drama.

This year, after reading the whole of Agatha Christie, I re-read Joseph Conrad's *The Secret Agent.* And to my astonishment I found myself longing for Agatha Christie's clean, declarative prose and straightforward narration. Conrad's fussy search for the *mot juste* was unnecessarily intrusive. His clumsy vocabulary was a stumbling block. His exaggerated search for profound psychological meaning in the pauses or gestures of extremely mundane characters did not give a convincing impression of depth. All these things interfered with the pace. The story, while based on fact, was not much less melodramatic than the better Agatha Christie novels. Only an infinitely superior conclusion showed the pen of a writer who had not formed bad habits in the popular marketplace. Yet it was clear that the same marketplace had given Agatha some good habits.

Agatha Christie's fellow professional crime writers never doubted her talent, indeed, her probable supremacy after Conan Doyle (always allowing for the exception taken by hard boiled writers). They could admire the easy flow of events which let the puzzle emerge. They could admire, too, the extraordinary ingenuity of some of those puzzles. Other writers might imagine curious routes to death, by injecting an air embolism or letting a man die of the noise in a belfry. But only Agatha Christie dared spring on her readers the surprise that the heroine was the murderer, or the hero was the murderer, or *all* the suspects were the murderer, or *all* the suspects were victims, *including* the murderer.

Hard boiled Raymond Chandler, sneering at the absurdity of one of Mrs Christie's most famous solutions, had to put behind him the justified criticism of his own work that the plots don't always make sense, and there is certainly no way that most readers could "detect" their way through a Raymond Chandler to come up with the "right answer". He is writing a different sort of book in which excitement for its own sake, coupled with a racier, more cynically witty prose than Agatha Christie's, offers quite different rewards.

Those who despised reading Christie by the end of her life might have noticed her friendship with Robert Graves. Although Graves could be outrageously pretentious and claim that he was a learned man writing valid history when he dredged through the worst scandalmongers of the ancient world to find copy for extravagant and sensational historical novels, he also knew that such novels were his bread and butter. He was a working writer, not – in prose – a dedicated artist with another occupation to make his living. And he did not despise a colleague who wrote unpretentious potboilers, never stooping to vulgarity or repulsive horror, never trotting out sexual sensation as spurious social observation.

Graves was most serious about his poetry. Although he often prated about inspiration, the Muse and "the White Goddess", the bulk of his commentary showed that he valued integrity above everything else in a poet. He disdained Eliot, Pound, Dylan Thomas and Yeats for their posturing – as he saw it. Agatha Christie never postured. She might fail, as she did when her undemanding and inoffensive poetry, printed at her own expense in the 1920s, remained unsold in Geoffrey Bles' warehouse for 40 years. But she didn't claim to be anything she wasn't, nor pretend to like or approve of things she didn't. Murder, she well understood, was merely a *donnée* in the whodunnit. Murderers were bad people, but not invariably the worst. The unforgivable offence was cruelty to children, too dreadful to write out in prose, but used as a mainspring of the plot offstage in the past in two of her plays after she had been extremely distressed by a reported case. Corrupting others with drugs or orgies was also unforgivable. But Agatha Christie wrote exciting puzzles, not moral lectures.

And as a writer of such she will be esteemed wherever the fashion for such puzzles survives.

AGATHA IN LATE MIDDLE AGE.

The Writer

In a cultivated home entertaining Kipling and Henry James, no wonder Clara Miller encouraged any signs of literary talent in her two daughters. Madge undoubtedly seemed the more promising. It is probable that for much of her life Agatha thought of herself as the secondary achiever in the shadow of her brilliant elder sister who had work in print before Agatha grew up, and a play on the stage when Agatha had only a detective novel and some short stories to point to.

Like most young writers, Agatha's earliest efforts were in poetry. Like most mature writers she came to dislike her early verse. She found it saccharine and insipid – but such was much Victorian and Edwardian taste. Still, poetry was a form she never abandoned. When she was earning enough to afford it, she paid Geoffrey Bles to print a collection of her poems. Creatively, she had been formed by the taste of her generation, and would always seem a post-Tennysonian with more of a Walter de la Mare than T.S.Eliot flavour to her work. Her own adult tastes, as occasionally mentioned in her writing, ranged from the quite demanding Yeats, (some of whose remoter pieces she expected a hero and heroine to be able to recognize) to the undemanding Frances Cornford (whose Fat White Woman Whom Nobody Loves Walking Through the Fields in Gloves was excessively anthologized to become one of those well-known poems that the cognoscenti may make a point of despising). If private poetry were measured like Sunday painting, however, Agatha Christie's pieces for her family would have to be adjudged perfectly reputable and by no means doggerel, even if they did not really merit publication. And she had a fine talent for private topical light verse.

Her avowedly serious writing her six "Mary Westmacott" novels and the play *Akhnaton* were, like her poetry, decent but forgettable. Eden Philpotts, the west country novelist and family acquaintance who generously advised her on her first adolescent attempt to write a novel, praised much of her creativity, and warned her to avoid passing moralistic authorial judgments. She took the advice. But if few people read Philpotts himself today, "Mary Westmacott" survives only because of Agatha Christie. Otherwise she would be completely lost in the lists of unread writers who can surprise with a jolt of memory when their names appear in publishers' lists at the back of secondhand books. The Warwick Deepings and Howard Springs and Crosby Garstins were probably better known than Westmacott in their day because they actually wrote better.

But Agatha Christie, once she had appeared under that name, was a writer who deserved to survive because of her supreme professionalism. She produced her manuscripts on time and to the correct length. Where sensible rewriting was required for sensible reasons, she undertook it without complaint. If the theatre required a play to have less characters or scenes, she understood and complied. She only dug her toes in when Hollywood wanted absurdities like Poirot in love. She yielded gracefully when the lucrative sale of her rights allowed Margaret Rutherford to travesty the character of Jane Marple. She was likely to prove sticky if confronted with a book jacket design she considered ugly or unseemly. But this in itself was sheer professionalism. The appearance of the volume in the shop mattered greatly to casual sales.

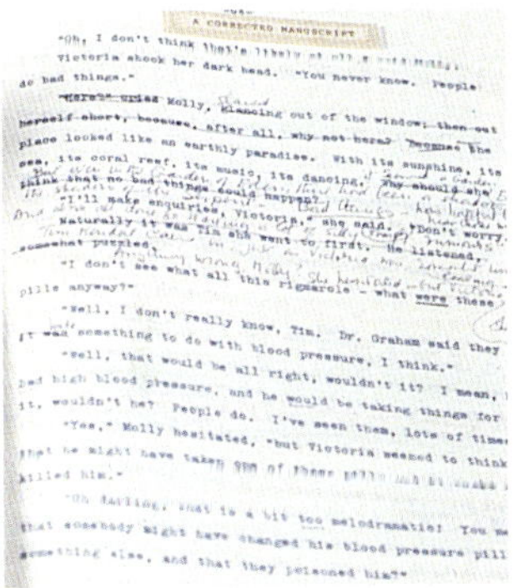
A CORRECTED MANUSCRIPT

"Oh, I don't think that's likely at all," ...
Victoria shook her dark head. "You never know. People do bad things."
~~"Here?" cried~~ Molly, glancing out of the window; then ... herself short, because, after all, why not here? ... place looked like an earthly paradise. With its sunshine, its sea, its coral reef, its music, its dancing. ... think that no bad things could happen?
"I'll make enquiries, Victoria," she said. "Don't worry."
Naturally it was Tim she went to first. He listened, somewhat puzzled.
"I don't see what all this rigmarole – what were these pills anyway?"
"Well, I don't really know, Tim. Dr. Graham said they ... it was something to do with blood pressure, I think."
"Well, that would be all right, wouldn't it? I mean, ... had high blood pressure, and he would be taking things for it, wouldn't he? People do. I've seen them, lots of times."
"Yes," Molly hesitated, "but Victoria seemed to think that he might have taken one of these pills and it ... killed him."
"Oh darling, that is a bit too melodramatic! You ... that somebody might have changed his blood pressure pill ... something else, and that they poisoned him?"

Her continuing need to write poetry and occasional serious novels betoken the spirit of the serious artist. It was her misfortune that like the Glastonbury composer she admired, Rutland Boughton, her talent did not match to to her temperament. It was her deserved success that steady application to the craft of making detective fiction brought her wealth and world-wide fame.

THE Unchanging World OF Cluedo

A handful of Agatha Christie's titles conjure up a familiar milieu. *The Body in the Library. The Murder at the Vicarage. A Murder is Announced. Murder on the Links.* As long as we don't mistake that Library for a municipal lending room, we see at once the secure upper middle class world of the interwar years. Golf is the recreation of choice, and to name the combination of greens, bunkers and fairways a golf *course* would be a horrid solecism. The vicarage is a place where we are welcome guests and social equals. The vicar's stipend may be less than the bank manager's salary, but with grand and draughty housing provided rent-free by the Church Commissioners he can hold up his head and offer sherry to the local gentry. We all have at least a parlourmaid, if not a butler, so that we don't answer the doorbell ourselves, but wait for our guests to be announced. We are not cramped for domestic space, with bookshelves lining our stairs and lavatories. We have a separate room designated the library, even if we don't do much more in there than look at the latest number of *Punch*, or consult an atlas before going on holiday.

SYMBOLS OF A BYGONE AGE: THE PARLOUR MAID AND THE CHIMNEY SWEEP.

We have no pretensions to being aristocracy. Our libraries don't attract visiting scholars. Our personal titles are professional or (retired) military – Dr or Col or Maj. Jane Austen and P.G.Wodehouse reassure us that the uppermost echelons of society are undesirable: Lady Catherine De Burgh patronizing the world from Rosings; fatuous asses frequenting the Drones Club. The lower orders may be ordinary and slightly comical, uttering the "servant galisms" with which *Punch* regales us. They may be "the salt of the earth": Cornish fishermen or forelock-touching policemen. They may be alarming outcasts: tramps and roughs and gypsies against whom the police will protect us. (They have to. The Chief Constable is always appointed from our number and, like the Assistant Commissioner at Scotland Yard, he is a social equal and a friend).

I've never lived like that. You probably haven't either. Maybe after 1914 no one was ever so secure from international anxieties, changing mores, or unwanted new housing ("ribbon development" in the interwar years). Yet that mythical world is instantly familiar and accessible and comfortable and we can easily imagine ourselves inhabiting it. Even if we usually eat in the kitchen, we can envisage moving between the breakfast room and the dining room to enjoy the best of the morning sunlight or the comfort of our candlelit refectory table. Even if we know we live more like Mr Pooter than Mr Bennett, we think of the latter as a possible friend and the former as some one to laugh at. Even if we are Icelandic or Polish or Australian, and reject with horror English class-consciousness, it seems we can enjoy the even tenor of that changeless world. At least we can enjoy its imperturbability when it is challenged by *The Body, The Murder, The Bloodstains, The Poison.* Agatha Christie, the mistress *par excellence* of the classic English murder mystery, has been read and enjoyed from China to Peru, translated into more languages than Shakespeare.

The contrast between the security of her settings and the understated shock and horror of her plot mainsprings seems to give her work universal appeal. If you or I come downstairs in the morning to find a stranger lying in the kitchen with a knife in his back, we shall have hysterics. If we hear that a friend or neighbour has had such an experience we shall be appalled and offer deeply embarrassed sympathy. But if we were Miss Jane Marple, we should murmur, "Now who could have done *that?*" and knit on without dropping a stitch.

Whodunnit? The classic question giving the spice of a puzzle to novels purveying an idealized picture of English middle class country life. There is no need for the Golden Age detective novelist to make the starting crime so vile that we instantly sympathize with the hero – a standard Dick Francis routine. There is no need for the victim to be so dislikable that we can't wait for him to be killed – unless that serves to increase the range of possible Suspects with a Motive. Our interest is *who* and *how.* As the board game Cluedo conveniently synopsizes a whole range of novels, was it Colonel Mustard with the gun in the dining room? Or the Reverend Green with the rope in the hall? Did Miss Scarlet confirm the wickedness of glamour by doing it with the knife in the library? Or did Mrs White contradict her lovable motherly appearance by using the lead pipe in the kitchen?

THE COSY ENGLISH VILLAGE, OFTEN AN ESSENTIAL ELEMENT IN CHRISTIE'S MURDER MYSTERIES.

The world of Cluedo suggests Agatha Christie more than any of her contemporaries. That cosiness and understated snobbery has done as much as anything to win her a vast audience and the contempt of intellectual critics.

And yet … and yet it surely misrepresents her? For this writer was as much at home in a Mesopotamian archaeological dig as in St Mary Mead. She and her characters travelled in search of the exotic on the Orient Express as willingly as the young Graham Greene. She loved the bone china securities of the prewar *rentier* classes as much as EM Forster hated them, yet the anti-Imperialist liberal critic of convention suffered spinsterly spasms and guilt over sexual improprieties which the middlebrow lady took in her stride.

An interesting lady. She worked in a literary convention as inflexible and artificial as pastoral poetry or Jacobean revenge tragedy. Yet she extended its territory, brought to it a touch of genius, and was, perhaps, the first truly lateral thinker in the form since Conan Doyle established it.

THE AMATEUR SLEUTHING GAME SO EVOCATIVE OF THE GOLDEN AGE OF THE DETECTIVE NOVEL.

Before Styles

In 1917 the 27-year-old VAD nurse working in the hospital pharmacy wrote her detective novel. Mrs Christie had been familiar with the genre for some time. Her own work would do more than anyone else's to define the Golden Age whodunnit. But she did not spring, fully-armed from the head of Zeus. She acknowledged predecessors, most often, most admiringly and most visibly Conan Doyle and his Sherlock Holmes.

Doyle, a general adventure story writer with a taste for the supernatural, had accidentally turned the detective story from a minor subdivision of popular fiction into a separate class of its own. Three of his four full-length Holmes novels show the detective introducing the mysterious conclusion of a London suspense thriller in an exotic setting – Utah, India and the Andamans, the Pennsylvania Shenandoah Valley – and in two of the three another hero plays a part, equal to and quite independent of Sherlock. The eccentric and omniscient brainbox, his mystifying deductions observed and described by an admiring middle-class everyman, proved overwhelmingly successful when featured in short stories for the *Strand* magazine. They spawned a host of imitators and established conventions.

SHERLOCK HOLMES : THE PROTOTYPE FICTIONAL DETECTIVE.

The Holmesian formula more often asks "why-he-dunnit?" or "he-dun-wot?" than "whodunnit?" The suspect is often obvious from the outset. But the villainous purpose of his mysterious actions remains for Holmes to unravel. Two years before Agatha Christie started writing, however, Doyle devised a truly brilliant plot to deceive the reader. In *The Valley of Fear*, the body whose murder Holmes investigates is not the person he and we imagine. In fact, it is the body of "the murderer" we think we are trailing, and clues to "the murderer's" identity are only read correctly by Holmes who silently perceives that (eg) the apparent extraordinary "removal" of the victim's wedding ring but replacement of the guard ring that sat above it really shows that the true owner of the rings placed one on the dead man's hand to mislead investigators, but could not bear to part with his own band of gold.

Doyle was still alive and producing Sherlock Holmes stories for the first 10 years of Agatha Christie's writing career. *The Casebook of Sherlock Holmes* appeared two years after *The Murder of Roger Ackroyd*. So Sherlock Holmes's greatest "howdunnit" story, *Thor Bridge*, in which elucidation of the method completely changes our perception of suspect and victim, could not have influenced her. Howdunnits were being brought to an extraordinary peak in Melville Davisson Post's *Uncle Abner* stories when Agatha embarked on her career, an extreme example being the explosion of a percussion cap in a locked room

ALEC GUINNESS AS FATHER BROWN.

by a liquor bottle so placed as to focus the sun's rays. It is unlikely that Agatha knew these American efforts when she started her own book. But she may well have been influenced by R. Austin Freeman, whose accurate knowledge of forensic pathology gave his "Dr Thorndyke" a realism (and a degree of dullness) never anticipated by the habitually inaccurate and inattentive Conan Doyle. She said she enjoyed the even duller Inspector West created by Freeman Wills Crofts: an inveterate student of railway timetables who used them to break alibis.

In fact, as GK Chesterton realized, the attraction of Holmes lay less in his pure detection than in his simple but arresting characterization. Chesterton effectively reversed the sleuth-like traits. A shabby little Catholic priest with a shovel hat, an untidy umbrella and the awkward habit of carrying everything in brown paper parcels, Father Brown looks the antithesis of hawk-eyed Holmes. Yet his knowledge of human nature, gleaned from hearing confessions, gives him a convincing edge over the rest of us. And Father Brown has his moments of observing and interpreting clues correctly, though time and again they turn out to be variants on Edgar Allen Poe's *The Purloined Letter*: something is best hidden by leaving it visible where it appears to be something else.

Poe does this with a document. Chesterton uses people. A postman on his round is disregarded by watchers looking for a mysterious visitor. A black man in a white country can disguise himself by putting on the burnt cork and white eyes of a minstrel show. A diner's feet seen under a screen may be taken for a waiter's since both wear evening dress. Agatha was to use variants of this trick repeatedly. Also, and less happily, Chesterton's insistence that Father Brown's profound knowledge of human weakness enables him to spot a criminal on psychological or spiritual grounds. In later years, Agatha's Miss Marple would be particularly given to psychological detection that didn't really add up. Even Poirot, her answer to Holmes, occasionally offered a piece of psychological deduction that you or I might just call a hunch.

And the hunch was becoming forbidden. Facetious Father Ronald Knox, who later drew up *Ten Commandments* for the detective story, insisted that it must be a puzzle which the detective worked out by interpreting tangible clues. Knox's cheek admitted a strong element of humour into the genre, as did Chesterton's old schoolfriend EC Bentley in his wildly over-rated *Trent's Last Case*, wherein the satirical idea that the detective should be wrong from start to finish creates neither good comedy nor good detection. But the licence to be funny in detective stories had been granted. Conan Doyle would take it up in *The Dying Detective*. Agatha Christie exploited it from the outset, without ever yielding to the temptation to let it take over her work.

Styles

WORLD WAR ONE, THE WESTERN FRONT: BARELY A MENTION OF THE WAR'S HORROR OCCURS IN AGATHA'S FIRST BOOK, THOUGH IT IS CLEARLY SET IN THIS TIME.

T*he Mysterious Affair at Styles* established Agatha Christie as a writer. It introduced Hercule Poirot and his Watson, Captain Hastings. It helped to set in concrete the Golden Age detective novel's preference for a country house setting where a large and varied group of suspects is assembled. It made the Christiean plotting talent's debut, misleading the reader by turning a reasonable and expected convention on its head. The detective proves the innocence of the likeliest culprit. But we never realize that this is because he believes him to be guilty, and does not want him to escape justice by coming to trial prematurely and winning an acquittal for lack of evidence.

Mrs Christie also showed off her pharmacy assistant's knowledge of poisons to great effect. There was probably no other detective writer on Earth who knew that the addition of bromide to a general tonic would precipitate the very small quantity of strychnine into a lethal dose at the bottom of the bottle, only to be taken after the rest of the medicine was finished. Nor that bromide delayed the action of strychnine, making the time of its ingestion difficult to determine. Thus the act of administering poison was brilliantly distanced from the time when the poison was taken. And a long spell of detection inviting the reader to work out who of the many people with an opportunity took the coffee cup to the murder victim proves a splendid misdirection. There was never any poison in the cup at all.

Disguises, red herrings and characters with other secrets and other reasons for administering drugs and creeping into strange bedrooms at night contributed to the mystery surrounding this classic locked room problem. A plan of the first floor of Styles was included: plans, diagrams and facsimiles of handwriting fragments had been used from time to time by Doyle, Knox and other detective writers. They usually established one point. Typically, Mrs Christie's explained two things. Equally typically, these things worked toward solving a subsidiary mystery, apparently incriminating yet actually eliminating a secondary suspect rather than pointing to the murderer.

She suggested that her murderers gave themselves away by over-egging the pudding: planting so many false clues that Poirot inevitably spotted them. She can be accused of the same thing herself. Styles house conceals altogether too many sub-plots. Marital jealousy and German espionage contribute misleading mysteries. Some things are heavily dressed up to look like clues – a young woman's amateur theatrical skill at transvestite disguise, for example. Actual clues to one of the subordinate mysteries are silently subsumed in the *donnée* that a character is a landgirl. The reader must grasp quickly that this means she's up before dawn for milking and her uniform includes a green armlet.

Another obvious mark of the inexperienced writer is the introduction of too many characters too quickly at the outset. When our narrator Captain Hastings comes to convalesce at his friend John Cavendish's Essex country house, he is immediately introduced to the occupants, who will become our principal suspects. Each in succession gets a couple of brisk paragraphs. Which does not fix them usefully in the reader's mind. Mrs Christie would soon overcome such simple technical faults. In fact, she showed in this book – above all with Poirot and Hastings – that she understood very well the value of creating a character by repeating a handful of memorable characteristics and not confusing the puzzle story with psychological profundity. A bit of a bounder has upset the family by marrying its wealthy matriarch for her money. His caddish outsider's personality is shown by his big black beard, heavy spectacles and patent leather shoes. One young woman is an orphan and a landgirl. Another is a nurse. Bold and simple strokes create boldly flat characters to sweep forward the all-important plot.

Données can look after themselves. The story is set in the present time, so there's a war on. Apart from the fact that young women are in occupations that would have been unthinkable for ladies in 1913, various patriotic fund-raisers happen offstage, and πa Polish Jew can be suspected of being a German spy, you would hardly know it. Rationing, cocoa-butter, Zeppelin raids and the sickening daily returns of casualties at the front never occur. Hastings's convalescence never suggests that his "Blighty" wound was very traumatic. His total silence about the horrors of the trenches in France is a mark of his creator's shallowness rather than his own insensitivity. The book is mercifully free from raging about "the Hun". Agatha was never seriously anti-German. But the apolitical quality that Mrs Christie's apologists delight in praising is really political naivety. Since the war gave her the chance to engage in enjoyable and positive work, its tragic role in European history is simply not noticed.

Equally, the matriarchal family set-up at Styles passes without comment. All the suspects are in some way dependent on Emily Cavendish's money. The character we never suspect moves away to an independent life, accusing them of being a set of sharks. But Agatha – herself married to a war hero who would later prove perfectly capable of supporting himself – never criticizes them; never suggests there is anything odd about these rather idly rich spongers. It was a useful situation to create a lot of murder suspects. She would use it again and again.

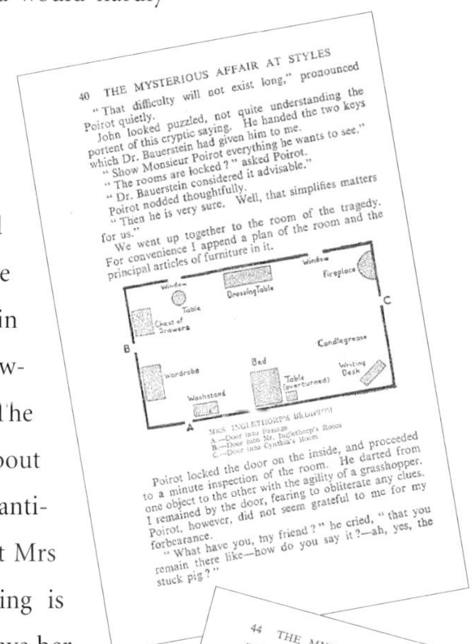
40 THE MYSTERIOUS AFFAIR AT STYLES

"That difficulty will not exist long," pronounced Poirot quietly.

John looked puzzled, not quite understanding the portent of this cryptic saying. He handed the two keys which Dr. Bauerstein had given him to me.

"Show Monsieur Poirot everything he wants to see."

"The rooms are locked?" asked Poirot.

"Dr. Bauerstein considered it advisable."

Poirot nodded thoughtfully.

"Then he is very sure. Well, that simplifies matters for us."

We went up together to the room of the tragedy. For convenience I append a plan of the room and the principal articles of furniture in it.

MRS. INGLETHORP'S BEDROOM
A.—Door into Passage
B.—Door into Mr. Inglethorp's Room
C.—Door into Cynthia's Room

Poirot locked the door on the inside, and proceeded to a minute inspection of the room. He darted from one object to the other with the agility of a grasshopper. I remained by the door, fearing to obliterate any clues. Poirot, however, did not seem grateful to me for my forbearance.

"What have you, my friend?" he cried, "that you remain there like—how do you say it?—ah, yes, the stuck pig?"

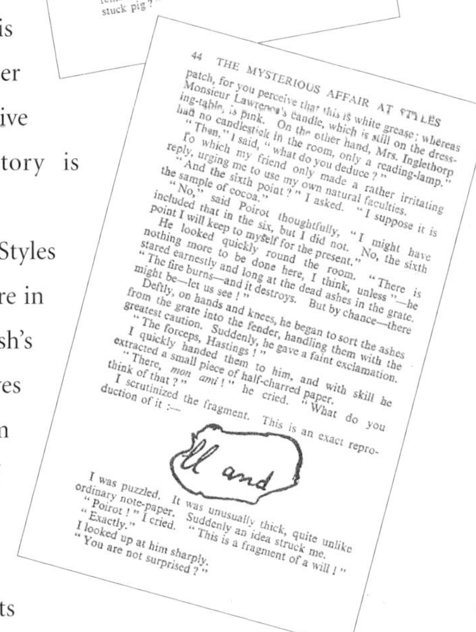
44 THE MYSTERIOUS AFFAIR AT STYLES

patch, for you perceive that this is white grease; whereas Monsieur Lawrence's candle, which is still on the dressing-table, is pink. On the other hand, Mrs. Inglethorp had no candlestick in the room, only a reading-lamp."

"Then," I said, "what do you deduce?"

To which my friend only made a rather irritating reply, urging me to use my own natural faculties.

"And the sixth point?" I asked. "I suppose it is the sample of cocoa."

"No," said Poirot thoughtfully, "I might have included that in the six, but I did not. No, the sixth point I will keep to myself for the present."

He looked quickly round the room. "There is nothing more to be done here, I think, unless"—he stared earnestly and long at the dead ashes in the grate. "The fire burns—and it destroys. But by chance—there might be—let us see!"

Deftly, on hands and knees, he began to sort the ashes from the grate into the fender, handling them with the greatest caution. Suddenly, he gave a faint exclamation.

"The forceps, Hastings!"

I quickly handed them to him, and with skill he extracted a small piece of half-charred paper.

"There, *mon ami*!" he cried. "What do you think of that?"

I scrutinized the fragment. This is an exact reproduction of it:—

I was puzzled. It was unusually thick, quite unlike ordinary note-paper. Suddenly an idea struck me.

"Poirot!" I cried. "This is a fragment of a will!"

"Exactly."

I looked up at him sharply.

"You are not surprised?"

AGATHA'S MANUSCRIPT OF THE MYSTERIOUS AFFAIR AT STYLES, WITH HOUSE PLAN AND HAND-WRITTEN CLUE.

Poirot

ALBERT FINNEY AS POIROT.

Following *Styles*, a couple of dozen short stories and a second novel, *The Murder on the Links*, fixed the characters of Hercule Poirot, his friend and narrator Captain Hastings, and his foil, Inspector Japp. Their ancestry was obvious. We are looking at Holmes, Watson and Lestrade with their external characteristics altered. There is even a Princess Romiroff to be Poirot's Irene Adler: the only woman he ever really admires.

Like Conan Doyle, Agatha appreciated the value of few repeated features to make her creation instantly recognizable. First, and most obviously, she distances her great detective from his environment by making him Belgian. And what are distinctively Belgian characteristics – apart from being a grateful refugee from the "Brave Little" Cockpit of Europe in 1917? Agatha really didn't know.

In fact, Poirot exhibits most of the stereotyped characteristics that conventional Englishmen of the day were supposed to despise in bourgeois Frenchmen. He is vain enough to dye his hair and moustache as he ages, and ultimately to replace them with wig and crepe hair. He is conceited, permanently expecting the world to have heard of him and admire him; cockily convinced that no one can get the better of Hercule Poirot's "little grey cells". He is too dapper by half, fussing about the dust-free perfection of his excessively smart suits and hats; torturing his feet with inappropriate and tight patent-leather shoes in the country. Although patent leather boots mark Arthur Inglethorpe as "a bounder" in *Styles*, Agatha wisely eschews the two supposed French habits which would have seemed particularly caddish to the English of her generation: Poirot does not trim his *embonpoint* with

DAVID SUCHET AS POIROT.

a corset, and does not use scent – which was only successfully purveyed to Englishmen under the euphemistic disguise of "aftershave lotion" toward the end of her life.

Poirot's taste in food is gallicized in ways to turn the stomach of a robust Englishman like Hastings. He drinks horrid *tisanes* instead of a nice cuppa tea; sickly *siropes* instead of whisky and soda; glutinous chocolate instead of breakfast coffee. How little Agatha knew or cared about the true nature of French cuisine is revealed when Poirot retires to cultivate vegetable marrows in *Roger Ackroyd.* A true Frenchman or Walloon would have shuddered at fattening up delicate courgettes into tasteless, watery, cotton-woolly monsters.

Poirot is short: something the tall Agatha (like the tall Thackeray before her) seems to have regarded as a mark of French inferiority. He has a head "exactly like an egg" – whatever that may mean. (He is certainly not as bald as an egg). Joseph Conrad, giving Sir Ethelred the Home Secretary an egg-shaped head in *The Secret Agent*, carefully specified that it rose from the heavy roundedness of his double chins. Agatha leaves us in doubt whether Poirot's head is big-end or little-end up, though she does repeatedly say he cocked it to one side. In later life she confessed that she herself had no idea what an egg-shaped head might be. Small wonder that actors from Charles Laughton to Peter Ustinov had the greatest difficulty in finding a convincing make up for Hercule Poirot!

The only supposed French characteristic Poirot signally lacks is erotic charm or success. Like Sherlock, he has a mind whose pure logicality will never be distracted by his hormones.

But all this superficially comic Frenchness serves three useful purposes. First, Poirot has an easily established voice: he speaks an English that sometimes literally translates simple French idioms. Then there is perpetual paradox. Poirot seems ridiculous at first sight. He does not command our instant respect, like Sherlock Holmes. So it is the more impressive when he proves to have been right all along. And finally, readers who have met him before will feel a sense of being in on the secret when new characters mistake him for a Frenchman, and Poirot declares indignantly that he is a Belgian.

His other great idiosyncrasy had a posthumous advantage that Agatha could hardly have anticipated. His irrational passion for symmetry and right angles in preference to curves harmonized his taste with the Art Deco

PETER USTINOV AS POIROT.

style of architecture and interior decoration which, influenced by Cubism and the post-Tutankhamun Egyptian style, dominated the late 1920s and 1930s. The man whose joy was complete when bakers started producing square crumpets became an apt ikon for the age of the Bauhaus and the chrome chair. Book designers and film makers came to see that Poirot stories offered a splendid vehicle for impressive period settings and ornamentation. Poirot's taste (introduced originally as a key to his spotting clues in asymmetrically disordered mantelpiece ornaments) made him a perfect exemplar of the period which coincided with detective fiction's golden age.

But all these characteristics add up to a flat character. No reading, chess-playing or intellectual hobbies provide grounding for the mighty intellect. No morality beyond a "bourgeois objection" to murder underlies his dedication to justice. No past police practice demonstrates the origin of his detective skills. He is easy to remember, but less entertaining than a Peter Wimsey; less human than a Father Brown; less awe-inspiring than a Sherlock. And this flatness contributed to intellectual misgivings about Agatha Christie's greatness, even at a time when the intelligentsia proudly admitted their addiction to whodunnits.

Hastings, AND OTHER Narrators

As befitted a writer whose childhood home entertained Henry James, Agatha always knew that fiction written without the clear focus of a narrative point-of-view could easily deteriorate into a "loose baggy monster". As befitted an acknowledged admirer of Conan Doyle, she copied the master in having an actual narrator to provide her first point of view. And she made her copying almost slavish by creating a narrator who was the Great Detective's Closest Friend; who was a model of convention and propriety to offset the Great Detective's eccentricities; who admired a pretty girl to offset the Great Detective's cerebral sexlessness; who plumed himself on his own detective skills, only to have his obtuseness mocked by the Great Detective; and who opened his first narrative during a return to England, invalided home after active service in the army. Had Captain Hastings been an army surgeon, the imitation of Dr Watson would have been obviously plagiaristic.

MONTY MILLER.

The rushed introduction of characters, at the outset of *Styles*, is carried over to Poirot himself, at least as regards his established friendship with Hastings. Quite how and when Hastings was ever in Belgium to meet this astonishingly talented police officer is never explained. Nor is it apparent why he should have become so closely friendly with a man whose character and habits are so far removed from his own. It is odder still that Poirot appears to have made no friends in his home country with whom he maintains any relations at all. It is surprising – or forgetful of Agatha – that the Captain Hastings who originally regaled the company at Styles with stories of Poirot's great detective achievements rapidly transmogrifies into a narrator who tries hopelessly to compete with the Great Brain. A couple of rather unsuccessful attempts to have Poirot narrate his own adventures to Hastings in short stories indicate that the good captain was outliving his usefulness, and, like Watson, was soon to be married off. Unlike Watson, he was to be banished to the Argentine, only to be called back periodically when his narrative voice seemed preferable to an omniscient creator.

Hastings – again like Watson – serves a secondary purpose of providing gentle comedy. In his case it is humour in the lightest feminist mould. Although Agatha never favoured organised feminism of any kind – not even the Women's Institute gets a mention in the idyllic village life of St Mary Mead – her sense of herself as a woman writer addressing herself to women readers is unmistakable. And Captain Hastings provides a gentle running satire on the masculinity of those officers and gentlemen the young Agatha surveyed as a pool for suitable husbands. His manners are impeccable. His gallantry is *sans peur et sans reproche*. But his eye for a pretty auburn-haired girl raises a knowing smile; his indignant denials of the attraction increase it; and his hearty self-confidence is treated with the affectionate amusement mothers bestow on their sons as they insist on their grown-up self-reliance.

HUGH FRASER AS CAPTAIN HASTINGS AND DAVID SUCHET AS POIROT.

It is a signal success that nowadays Captain Hastings can still amuse women in the supposed age of sexual equality, though Agatha wisely abandoned him altogether after the early 1940s as she sensed World War Two had finally dissipated that society of privileged, manipulating dependent women of which she so much approved. Male readers are always less likely to see or enjoy the joke. Hastings' obtuseness compared with Poirot's feline and feminine sensitivity will probably seem to them too bluntly and crudely overdrawn. And their wives and sisters and mothers can again smile affectionately at their proving the success of Agatha's kindly caricature of masculine foibles.

Well before the dismissal of Hastings, Agatha had recognized the usefulness of a narrator or main character supplying the point-of-view who was *not* used as comic relief. Quasi-investigators, either alongside the featured detective or acting on their own recur: Anne Beddingfield in *The Man in Brown Suit*, Jerry Burton in *The Moving Finger*, Charles Hayward in *The Crooked House*. Mr Satterthwaite's point of view always mediates Harley Quin's insights for us, and once combines with Poirot in *Murder in Three Acts*. Most interestingly, Nurse Leatheram in *Murder in Mesopotamia* is a narrator who combines Agatha Christie's sterling good sense and nursing-derived practicality with a lower-middle-class Philistinism and dubious grammar which may be interpreted as either the author's snobbery or as a humorous caricature of her own supposed "lowbrow" appearance in the rarefied academic world of Max and the Woolleys.

The Man in the Brown Suit alternates Anne's point of view with Sir Eustace Pedler's diary: the first and most light-hearted use of the villain's or apparent villain's point-of-view. Variants of this technique would be used repeatedly with immense skill: controversially in *The Murder of Roger Ackroyd*; subtly in *The ABC Murders*; unobtrusively in *Death in the Clouds*; penetratingly in *Endless Night*.

Five Little Pigs is a *tour de force* of narrative construction, with all the suspects plausibly giving their own accounts of the catastrophe, so that we know we are looking for the one who is lying. And narrators like the Reverend Len Clement, Sir Edward Palliser KC and Miss Marple herself (in *Miss Marple Tells a Story*) invite the realization of characters through their narrative voices which is, perhaps, only surpassed in Nurse Leatheram.

Early Directions

Three of the next four novels Agatha Christie wrote were thrillers rather than whodunnits, though the distinction was not so clearcut in the age of Edgar Wallace and Dornford Yates as it is in the age of Jack Higgins and Margaret Yorke. Like *The Secret Adversary* (1922), *The Man in the Brown Suit* (1924), and *The Secret of Chimneys* (1925), Agatha's later thrillers would always contain some element of mystery to be solved and usually some master villain to be identified from among a range of suspects.

Usually, too, the master-villain's web would weave together "leftists" and "traitors". Mr Brown, the secret adversary, is the master-criminal behind the Bolsheviks who is plotting the disaster of a Labour government. His people organized the pro-Boer anti-war feeling in 1899–1902, and pacifist propaganda from 1914–1918. Both Sinn Fein and Unionist agitators are in his pay, along with most Labour MPs. The villain of *The Man in the Brown Suit* aims to provoke revolution in South Africa. The Brotherhood of the Red Hand plots bloodcurdling republican revolution in *Chimneys*, and are foiled by a man so "democratic" that he never uses his title, but happily accepts an offer to be King of Herzoslovakia.

All her life Agatha would tend to equate Communists with pacifists, and imagine both to be pro-German traitors. When her anti-Semitic propensity is added to the mix, her political naivety seems pretty repellent. But it should be remembered that she is almost the only naive right-winger of her generation whose opinions are still widely read, and that they were, to some extent, shared by others like the brilliant Lord Chancellor F.E. Smith and the odious anti-Semitic, anti-Communist, paranoid spy maniac, Scotland Yard assistant commissioner Sir Basil Thomson.

Thomson's scandalous downfall, trying to lie his way out of arrest for public indecency with a prostitute in Hyde Park, contrasts with a far more appealing side of the young Agatha. Her thrillers feature active, energetic young heroines who have shaken off the long skirts and prudish shackles of Edwardian convention. Prudence Cowley, accosted by one of the Secret Adversary's minions in the park, is no innocent young miss. She thinks indignantly that she has been mistaken for a prostitute. Like short-skirted Anne Beddingfeld in *The Man in the Brown Suit*, and *Chimneys*' "Bundle" Brent in a later reincarnation, she is praised for her legs and ankles.

"THE DISASTER OF A LABOUR GOVERNMENT": A FRENCH JOURNAL IMAGINATIVELY EXAGGERATES THE SHOCK OF SOCIALIST PRIME MINISTER RAMSAY MACDONALD ATTENDING A *LEVÉE* IN COURT DRESS.

Agatha always delighted in lively young women with a ready wit and intelligent independence. They might be upper-class girls with cheeky nicknames like "Bundle". Equally they might be young women with no money behind them and their way to make in the world, like Victoria Jones in *They Came to Baghdad* or Lucy Eylesbarrow in *4.50 from Paddington*. Prudence "Tuppence" Cowley combines both qualities. In thrillers, their adventures usually include kidnap by the villains. In either thrillers or whodunnits, they often enjoy the support of older, wiser heads: Miss Marple's for Lucy, while strong, silent Colonel Race of the Secret Service makes his first appearance in *The Secret Adversary*.

But if Agatha set a pattern for later thrillers in her first few years of writing, the 29 short stories featuring Poirot and Hastings, and the novel *Murder on the Links*, established the whodunnit mode in which she would become supreme. Like Sherlock Holmes, the Poirot of the stories is not confined to catching murderers. He solves the mysteries behind fraud cases. He catches jewel thieves. (Indeed, the ubiquitous jewel thief, working alone or in a gang, would become a frequent red herring suspect in Agatha's later work). He exposes blackmailers. Once, in "The Missing Will", he and Hastings simply play an elaborate game of hunt-the-slipper in an old farm house: not a who-dun-it; just a where-is-it that may have puzzled readers who expected crime fiction to be about crime.

Agatha's preferred motives for murder were established early in her career. Avarice is first and foremost. Over and over again, her murderers seek to inherit by killing. And their victims have several potential heirs, providing a choice of suspects. Killing a blackmailer, or killing to preserve a guilty secret is her next preferred motive. And revenge or sexual jealousy are occasionally admitted. Like all other "soft-boiled" writers, she rigorously eschews the commonest causes of actual homicide: domestic quarrels or drunken mayhem. Nor does she admit organized crime's professional hitmen as a rule, though "The Adventure of the Cheap Flat" combines an ingenious reversal of Conan Doyle's device in "The Three Garridebs" with something like a recollection of his Mafia-related "The Red Circle".

"The Cheap Flat" may also owe something to the activities of the "House Spider"; an actual fraudster who offered flats at absurdly low rentals then absconded with premiums and first payments from would-be tenants. Agatha glanced at the true crimes in the news throughout her career. She based *Murder on the Links* on a French case where intruders tied up a wife and killed her husband.

SIR ARTHUR CONAN DOYLE, INSPIRATION FOR SOME OF AGATHA'S SHORT STORIES.

And she was almost cruelly tactless in "The Affair at the Victory Ball", echoing the death of actress Billie Carleton from an overdose of cocaine after just such a dance. Happily on this occasion she did not imitate the xenophobia with which the police and press pursued Chinese drug-dealer Brilliant Chang. Her murderous dope pedlars were an English couple.

THE Murder OF Roger Ackroyd

"Who Cares who Killed Roger Ackroyd?" was the great American critic Edmund Wilson's famous question, as he laid into detective fiction in general and Agatha Christie in particular in 1944. The question showed that a great many people did. Enough people recognized *Roger Ackroyd* for it to supply a generic term for the whodunnit. For it is impossible to discuss the controversial device by which this novel established Agatha's reputation and sales without revealing the mystery. IF YOU HAVEN'T READ THE BOOK AND WISH TO TRY AND SOLVE THE MYSTERY, TURN THE PAGE AT ONCE AND MOVE ON.

EDMUND WILSON.

As a matter of fact – and diffidently disputing Edmund Wilson's judgment – I found the book fascinating and suspenseful even though I knew whodunnit before I read it. With full knowledge of the murderer's identity from the outset, I was puzzled to see how the denouement could have been plotted. Reading this book really was like watching an expert conjuror. I knew a trick was being perpetrated. I knew the basic principle. Yet, watching closely, I couldn't see how it was being done. So when I had read it, I was fully equipped to enter the debate this book engendered among Agatha's admirers. Did she cheat? Was it, as the *Daily Sketch* claimed, "the best thriller ever" in 1926? Or was the *News Chronicle* right to call it "a tasteless and unfortunate letdown"?

The letdown (if there is one) is not the sort of silly evasion that has several months' episodes of a television soap suddenly written off as a dream, or two-thirds of a Denis Wheatley black magic thriller suddenly revealed to have taken place "on the astral plane", so that the plot never really occurred. The letdown lies at the heart of the original suggestions behind the novel. Madge's husband James casually remarked that he had never seen a novel in which the Watson character turned out to be the murderer. Agatha said that it would be technically very difficult – and since her mind presumably turned at once to Captain Hastings, she might have added well-nigh impossible without jarring that honest and upright character into total insanity.

But a letter from Lord Louis Mountbatten, sent via the *Daily Sketch*, offered roughly the same technical challenge. He proposed having the narrator as the surprise murderer, his alibi being that he was with the detective at the time of the murder, and that the detective himself might be suspected. To show ways in which it might be done, he enclosed a synopsis in a sequence of letters between Poirot, Hastings and the murderer. And he invited Agatha to make use of it, as his busy naval life would never allow him the time.

Agatha acknowledged the letter, and wisely dropped the outmoded suggestion of a novel in letters. She also dropped Hastings altogether, introducing a Poirot who has retired to King's Abbot near Cranchester, with the intention of raising vegetable marrows. And her narrator, Dr Sheppard, attaches himself to Poirot, reporting on the way the Great Detective is finding clues and tracing suspects.

The mystery is in the classic form of the "locked room". Rich Roger Ackroyd is stabbed in his study. Dr Sheppard was his last known visitor and he tells people that Ackroyd had sent for him to reveal that a recently deceased lady committed suicide because she was being blackmailed. He says Ackroyd received the name of the blackmailer – presumably also the murderer – in a letter. Ackroyd is heard talking to somebody inside the room half an hour after Dr Sheppard has left the house.

The way in which Dr Sheppard managed his alibi was technically perfectly proper – if a little unconvincing given the quality of mechanical sound reproduction in the 1920s – and described by critics as something that should not be repeated. As far as traditional detection problems went, this was the heart of the plot, as was recognized when the book was dramatized under the title *Alibi*. Sheppard's lie about the blackmailer is a permissible murderer's lie. But the controversial deception was purely literary. If we learn the story from Dr Sheppard, and know his thoughts and reactions, surely they must have been distorted for us to think him innocent? It was a "commandment of crime fiction", as drawn up by Ronald Knox, that the murderer's thoughts must never be shown to suggest that he knows himself to be innocent. (Just such a "thought" clue enables the reader to eliminate a strong suspect in the 1922 thriller *The Secret Adversary).* Agatha and her defenders insist that she didn't cheat: Dr Sheppard concealed some thoughts, but did not distort those he revealed. Agatha's accusers maintain that such equivocation amounts to distortion, and the circumstances by which Sheppard writes us his account before his suicide are unconvincing and contribute to the sense of letdown. I personally incline to agree with the prosecution, while thinking it a storm in a teacup to complain of authorial manipulation in a work of pure entertainment, which, I admit, entertains anyway!

CHARLES LAUGHTON AS HERCULE POIROT IN *ALIBI.*

Fudged or brilliant, *The Murder of Roger Ackroyd* was the making of the Queen of Crime. Although sales were not extraordinary, her name was well enough known to merit silly-season headlines when her 11-day disappearance occurred at the end of the year. The disappearance brought her books still more publicity. From 1926, her sales rose steadily and never looked back.

Scrambling

SHERLOCK HOLMES LEAPS TO THE RESCUE, DISGUSED AS A FRENCH LABOURER.

Even before Archie acknowledged his love for Nancy, Agatha's fiction revealed a mind in turmoil about marriage. The short story "Magnolia Blossom" first appeared in *Royal Magazine* in 1925. It tells of a wife who loyally aborts her elopement from her smarmy husband on hearing that his firm is collapsing, only to find that he is deliberately trying to prostitute her to her lover in order to recover papers which would lead to his conviction for embezzlement. So she leaves them both and accepts renunciation and loneliness.

The story is intensely bittersweet and a far cry from the happy flirtatious Edwardian girl in search of Mr Right. It touches on the perception that upper-class marriage for money is morally indistinguishable from prostitution. It places an enormous premium on loyalty, as the wife punishes herself for having been the unwitting pawn of a plot to exploit her lover. It indulges the gratifying corollary that even a manipulative husband probably *feels* intense passion for the wife he so misuses that he deservedly loses her. "Magnolia Blossom" suggests that Agatha felt obscurely abandoned before things had come into the open. And her response was to retreat into a passionate belief in her own morality of openness as more important than chastity, and a helpless self-deception that *really* Archie's love for her could never die, no matter howbadly he behaved.

Once the marriage had positively collapsed, her inner turmoil became so great that she could hardly write, and she produced some of her worst fiction. *The Big Four*, the novel strung together on Campbell Christie's advice from the *Daily Sketch* series of Poirot stories, is surely the very worst novel she ever wrote: worse than the geriatric dodderings of *The Postern of Fate* and *Elephants Can Remember*. Though there are traces of the most ingenious of all whodunnit composers – poison can be found in yellow jasmine flowers: a Ruy Lopez opening in chess compels a certain responding move which may be exploited to trigger an infernal device – the book as a whole is an incoherent mixture of elements drawn from Conan Doyle, Sax Rohmer, Edgar Wallace and "Sapper". The Doylean elements, too, are liable to be those least suitable for translation to the sedentary and dandyish Poirot. When he and Hastings disguise themselves as French workmen, totally deceiving the opposition, one recalls Holmes astonishing Watson with an identical disguise. Poirot is unconvincing as a man of action and athleticism, toting a gun. His "death" and rebirth as his identical twin brother Achille are unworthy of a *Boys' Own Paper* yarn. The fiendish Chinese villain, capable of devilish tortures, is a dire borrowing from inferior thriller writers, and his Limehouse oubliette strongly suggests that Agatha never got nearer the East End than the pages of other sensational writers. Even the pace, normally one of Agatha's

DR. FU MANCHU: THE CLASSIC FIENDISH "HEATHEN CHINESE".

great strengths, is all over the place in this dreadful book. Reviewers rightly hated it.

It is the more remarkable that Agatha reserved her own especial hatred for her next novel, *The Mystery of the Blue Train*. She correctly observed that it marked her emergence from the chrysalis as a fully-fledged professional writer, since she soldiered on to complete it after she had lost interest, as well she might in the aftermath of her marital breakdown. She wrongly thought it was therefore laboured and boring. It is in fact an excellent reworking of the short story "The Plymouth Train". Agatha may have felt that the telling became too stolidly workmanlike after the excellent opening contrasts between dangerous Apache-haunted Paris back streets, and the unendurable over-privileged set on the French Riviera. There are also a couple of generalizations about women that do not live up to the insightfulness of her usual homespun wisdom. She suggests that all women find jewels irresistible, and apparently believes in the innocent maiden's dream that the love of a good woman may reform a bounder. At the same time, however, she introduced an unusual pro-Semitic generalization – Jews are a race who will never forget a kindness. And she revived the sympathetic Jewish background character Joe Aarons, who had appeared in *The Big Four*. A new background figure who would recur whenever Poirot needed an active investigative agent was the shadowy Mr Goby.

Two 1929 novels reviving earlier young thriller protagonists marked a decline. "Bundle" Brent was given a more central role in *The Seven Dials Mystery*. She and her set – including a perfect 1929-type girl called "Socks" who works the word "subtle" to death – are even more PG Wodehouse-y than they had been in *The Secret of Chimneys*, and rather less inclined to toss out disparaging remarks about Jews, "Dagoes" and "Niggers". The location of Seven Dials itself baffled Agatha completely. She once placed it roughly correctly "near Tottenham Court Road" in the West End of London, but most of the time imagined it to be in the East End. The plot seems indebted to Chesterton's *The Man Who Was Thursday*.

P.G. WODEHOUSE.

Tuppence Cowley, now married to her co-star Tommy Beresford, also appeared in *Partners in Crime*. Like *The Big Four*, this followed an unhappy structure in which a chase for a central villain was subsumed in a series of unrelated short stories. The parodies of different fictional detective writers have delighted some readers, but leave others cold, especially as many of the originals are now forgotten.

Settling

In 1934 Agatha wrote *Murder on the Orient Express.* Her phase of creative uncertainty was over and done with. Once again, as she had done in *Ackroyd,* the greatest of all literary prestidigitators pulled off an absolutely new and unique illusion. Henceforth she had to be acknowledged the Queen of Crime.

But it had been clear over the previous four years that she had recovered her form. In 1930 she created three new and lasting characters: Mr Harley Quin with his mediator, Mr Satterthwaite, and the lady who would ultimately outshine Poirot as the reflection of Agatha Christie's England: Miss Jane Marple. In 1934 Mr Parker Pyne joined her creations. And with that, the roster of Mrs Christie's recurring centre-stage detectives was complete. Mrs Ariadne Oliver, after working for Parker Pyne, is always cast as the friend and associate of Poirot. Colonel Race, Superintendent Battle, and the whole gamut of inspectors and chief inspectors are always supporting some more prominent investigator or adventurer. So are those chief constables whose names (Melchett, Melrose, Johnson) seem to recur as their forces mysteriously alter (Yorkshire, Downshire, Middleshire and unnamed locales resembling either Devonshire or unspecified parts of the home counties or west country).

LAUREN BACALL AS THE BRAINS BEHIND *THE MURDER ON THE ORIENT EXPRESS.*

Not all the newly created protagonists were of equal merit. And some who never appeared in second novels might have been worth reviving. Bobby Jones and Lady "Frankie" Derwent, for example, of *Why Didn't They Ask Evans?* (1933), appeal to some readers more than the comparable Tommy and Tuppence Beresford or "Bundle" with her boyfriend Bill Eversleigh. Emily Trefusis of *The Sittaford Mystery* (1931) is a truly interesting example of the quick-witted and independent-minded young Christiean heroine, displaying quite idiosyncratic features of Agatha's feminine-feminist thinking. For with all her heroine's charm and vitality, Emily categorically prefers as her lover the least heroic of all the young men in the book; a wet character who would be constantly in trouble did she not keep a firm eye on him. Yet she easily dominates and sexually manipulates every male she meets, and may surprise the reader as much as the character when she decisively rejects the positive young journalist who has helped with her detective work, and declares her constant love for hopeless John Pearson.

Indeed love, which seemed to have treated Agatha so scurvily, became one of the more interesting details of her backgrounds. The relationship between Bobby and

THE SITTAFORD MYSTERY: A SUCCESS SET IN AGATHA'S FAMILIAR DARTMOOR.

Lady Frankie is interestingly and convincingly constrained by the sense that she is an earl's daughter and he a vicar's son, who was a suitable playmate when they were children, but may be less acceptable in the role of suitor. The Reverend Len Clement, narrator of *Murder at the Vicarage*, is given a slightly stuffy parsonical voice, to let us wonder – wrongly – whether his passionate love for his very unparsonical and 20-years-younger wife is fully reciprocated. Another vicar's wife, Mrs Dane Harmon, enjoys the strange nickname "Bunch", for what Mrs Christie tells us is "the obvious reason". It wasn't instantly obvious to me, and Mrs Christie kindly explained in the later novel *A Murder is Announced* (1950) that it described her roundness of face and figure. Which reminded me that the only girl I ever knew with that nickname was given it with reference to her generous and often exposed cleavage. Again, Agatha firmly places happy and legitimate sexual attraction squarely in the parsonage.

In *Sad Cypress*, Agatha had the courage to re-create imaginatively the anguish of sexual jealousy. The pain may have caused the peculiar hiccups in the book: the victim's stepfather is called Ephraim in the early chapters, but has become Bob when his deceased wife's letter explaining Mary's birth is found. Mary herself was born illegitimate before World War One: parts of the plot turn on this detail. Yet she declares herself to be 21 years old in 1929, her parents having married in 1919 when she was one year old.

But these minutiae, like occasional clues which are never fully followed up and explained, do not detract from the success of the book. The puzzle, always Agatha's prime concern, is fairly presented and can be solved. And this had become the keynote of her writing once again. She dropped the silly stringing together of short stories into a poor imitation of picaresque structure. If she wanted to write a sequence of short stories, she did so. If she wanted to indulge in mooniness, mysticism or horror, she revived earlier work, so that the collection *The Hound of Death* contains some curious supernatural horror stories; some mystical juvenilia; and one of Agatha's most successful pieces of surprise plotting: *Witness for the Prosecution.*

AGATHA CHRISTIE AT THE HEIGHT OF HER POWERS IN 1933.

The early 1930s were marked by Agatha's faintly amused observation of the importance otherwise sensible people attached to spiritualist seances, and her return to outstanding puzzle-plotting. *Why Didn't they Ask Evans?* Well, they didn't fail in the way you probably expect, nor was Evans the person you probably imagine. The sentence is perfectly worded to convey its intended meaning, yet without the context neither "ask" nor "Evans" carries its obvious denotation. *The Sittaford Mystery, Murder at the Vicarage, Peril at End House, Lord Edgware Dies*: any two of the novels Agatha wrote between 1930 and 1934 would have made the name of a lesser writer. Truly she had entered into her own golden age.

The Beresfords

Tommy and Tuppence Beresford spanned Agatha's creative life. They were hero and heroine of the second novel she wrote, and hero and heroine of the last. Most of Agatha's recurring protagonists were granted the wisdom of maturity or elderliness from their inception. The Beresfords were a bright young couple bravely facing a postwar world of limited employment possibilities in 1922. Unlike Agatha's other bright young protagonists ("Bundle" Brent, Emily Trefusis, Jerry Burton of *The Moving Finger*), they were resuscitated four times, until they were an old couple living largely on their memories in *The Postern of Fate* (1974).

Agatha evidently felt strong affection for them. Tuppence's maiden name, Cowley, echoes the model of Morris car that gave young Agatha so much pleasure and such a sense of adventure. *By the Pricking of My Thumbs* (1968) is dedicated to "the many readers in this and other countries who write to me asking: 'What has happened to Tommy and Tuppence? What are they doing now?'"

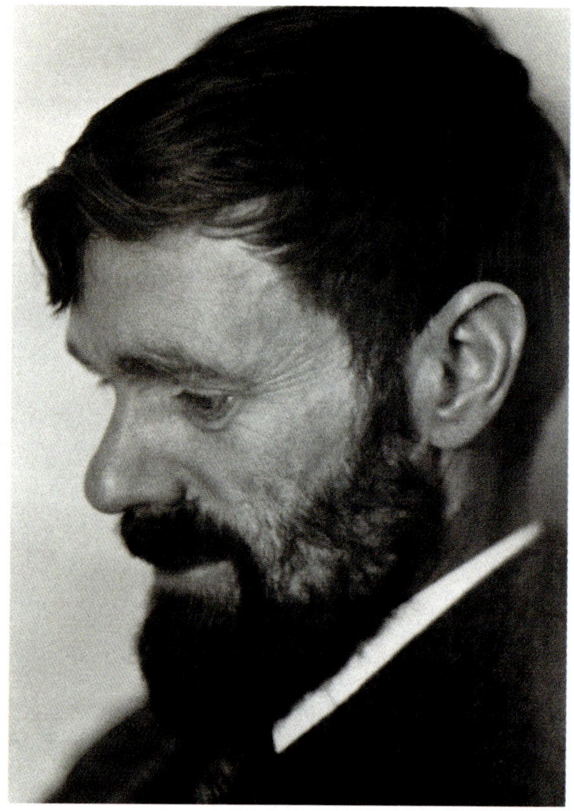

D.H. LAWRENCE – "I LIKE THE MEN AND WOMEN OF MY GENERATION".

This affection might be explained by their being the characters through whom she found success in the thriller: a genre she found easier to write than the whodunnit. But a more obvious source of their appeal is their contemporaneity with her. She had created in Hercule Poirot a slightly comic elderly foreigner. She had created in Captain Hastings, a decent but limited young fogy. Tommy and Tuppence were lively, decent young people with a sense of fun. Like D.H. Lawrence – and most other people – she "liked the men and women of her generation". Although Tommy and Tuppence are about 10 years younger than Agatha – Tuppence, for example, enjoys the short skirts of 1929 which show off girls' legs and her own trim ankles – they share her pleasure in the postwar modernity which shocks their elders. Tuppence is equally delighted by cloche hats and bobbed hair which obviate the need for hairpins. Their sense of fun has a very precise youthful interwar contemporaneity. The postcards they interchange as a secret code are Bonzo cartoons: the smiley dog who delighted young people between 1920 and 1940. They make lightly teasing reference to old Sir Arthur Conan Doyle's embarrassing belief that he had seen real photographs of real fairies.

They tease each other merrily, too. Their infectious pleasure in each other's company leads them to remark on the sex appeal of other people, and Tuppence in particular likes to joke about Tommy's noticing other girls' attractions, or young girls having "a pash" for him.

But their sense of fun has always annoyed their detractors. "Insufferably high-spirited" is a common description of these two, who call each other, "old bean" and "old thing" and dismiss compliments and serious sentiment with a hasty, "rot!" When some of their adventures were televised in the 1960s, a younger generation wondered disbelievingly what was supposed to be the attraction of this natty pair who were so inexplicably pleased with themselves. By the time they reached old age, their banter was self-indulgent maundering, impeding the plot without offering any entertainment to anyone who wasn't a longstanding Beresfords fan or contemporary.

Since they feature largely in spy thrillers, they inevitably utter some of Agatha's extraordinary political prejudices. But their high spirits reach an intolerable pitch when they rejoice in the idea of world war. The war was "the good old days" they agree in 1929. He enjoyed driving a General bus. She imagines that he was surrounded by pretty nurses. Worse still in 1940, Tommy chants, "The blitzkrieg is coming, hurrah! hurrah!" and looks forward to some more active intelligence service. Their highest ideal in middle age is the memory of Nurse Edith Cavell's, "Patriotism is not enough; I must have no hatred or bitterness for anyone." Their full awareness of the last sentence lifts their admiration of the propaganda saint above the crude use to which she was put by the allies, who represented her perfectly legitimate execution for helping British and Belgian soldiers escape from German occupation as an excellent reason to Hate the Hun. But Tommy and Tuppence also seem to interpret it as meaning that while the Nazis have overstepped the mark a bit, only "skunks" refuse to fight for their own country.

PROPAGANDA EXPLOITATION OF THE EXECUTION OF NURSE CAVELL.

Nostalgia for the war probably identifies the importance of the Beresfords to Agatha. Their affectionate matiness, lightly charged with erotic appeal, is well realized from the outset, and surely must have been based on her relations with Archie. He had always used facetiousness to mask the horrors of war. He had always shared Agatha's wish to live adventurously. And even after he had left her life and Agatha was happily married to a man 14 years younger, it seems she daydreamed about living on to old age with the man of her own generation. To me, Agatha's treatment of Tommy Beresford is very reminiscent of Margaret Mitchell's nostalgia for her drunken and abusive first husband: the sexy Rhett Butler of *Gone with the Wind*. Her second supportive husband could only be the decent Ashley Dukes.

And Tuppence is the young, happy, daredevil person with few responsibilities who lives on inside us all, and has no wish to mistake pomposity for wisdom.

CLARK GABLE AND VIVIEN LEIGH AS RHETT BUTLER AND SCARLETT O'HARA: MARGARET MITCHELL'S IDEALIZATION OF HER UNSUCCESSFUL FIRST MARRIAGE.

Mr Harley Quin AND Mr Parker Pyne

HARLEQUIN AND PANTALOON FROM EARLY NINETEENTH-CENTURY AUSTRIA.

The Harlequinade delighted Agatha from her childhood. Auntie-Grannie owned porcelain figurines of the traditional characters: Harlequin and Columbine, Pierrot and Pantaloon. Agatha loved them, and she introduced them into her early story "The Affair at the Victory Ball". And in the melancholy mood that followed her marital breakdown, she invented the magical character of Mr Harley Quin.

Her Harley Quin stories are a sport. All but "The Harlequin Tea Set"are included in the collection *The Mysterious Mr Quin.* Agatha usually kept her half-sceptical interest in the paranormal out of her fiction. In the Harley Quin stories she indulged it creatively, inventing an other-worldly character who turns up unexpectedly and who, by some trick of the light, normally seems at first sight to be wearing Harlequin's brilliant body-suit.

Mr Quin gives hints about past crimes or future dangers to wealthy 62-year-old Mr Satterthwaite: a man who has always been in the background of high society but who, under Mr Quin's coaching, makes penetrating observations on mysteries confronting his temporary company, and thereby either solves crimes or prevents catastrophes. Usually these involve helping a pair of lovers who are threatened. Often Mr Quin reappears to insist that it was Mr Satterthwaite's percipience that really saved the day.

Mr Quin is a mediocre but adequate fantasy figure, of no great interest except insofar as his concern for young lovers – like that occasionally evinced by Hercule Poirot – is a mark of Agatha's appealing sentimentality: a generally benign approval of other people's happy emotions, without any great penetration.

Mr Satterthwaite is rather more interesting. A rich, elderly sedentary man, his background allows Agatha to make tactful use of her own quite discriminating and advanced artistic taste. Her normative characters like paintings depicting something real and natural by

WYNDHAM LEWIS, FOUNDER OF THE VORTICIST SCHOOL OF PAINTING THAT AGATHA ADMIRED.

painters like Lord Leighton or Edwin Landseer, Mr Satterthwaite not only enjoys vorticist painting (the post-cubist style perpetrated by Wyndham Lewis), but he quietly observes the balance and proportion which mark the best of a collection. In Agatha's authorial voice, such observations would have seemed off-putting and high-brow. When her contemporary Denis Wheatley attempts to exhibit his upper-class protagonists' fine taste he usually seems hifalutin and culturally pig-ignorant. When Dorothy Sayers adds half-baked scholarship and connoisseurship to Lord Peter Wimsey's preposterous range of physical and mental talents, we are not convinced. But when Agatha offers the understated but intelligent opinions of a gentleman who is usually more concerned that his money should secure him first-class travel and good hotel rooms, there is not a hint of showing off on the part of author or character.

And Agatha's commonsense morality is exhibited in the treatment of Mr Satterthwaite's weakness: his snobbery. He loves the company of duchesses and deservedly distinguished celebrities. And why not? Since he doesn't look down his nose at inferiors, and his manners are excellent in any company, his foible is not culpable. Agatha's sense of personal (as opposed to social or political) morality is normally very sound. And Mr Satterthwaite deserved his later outing away from Mr Harley Quin but in company with Hercule Poirot in *Three Act Tragedy*.

Mr Parker Pyne is another elderly observer who has acquired Wisdom. Paradoxically, his observation has been restricted to Civil Service files. But Administrative Grade Civil servants usually have first class minds to match their first class degrees, and he is a perfectly plausible Wise Old Gentleman. The original twist to the first seven Parker Pyne stories is the idea that he knows the five causes of human unhappiness, and can, for a fee that fluctuates with his clients' means, make people happy again. He doesn't tell us what the causes are, but two of them are evidently sexual jealousy and boredom. Parker Pyne employs a professional gigolo and a vamp, with actors hired for special occasions, to plunge his clients into adventures which win back their straying spouses or lift their general depression or anxiety. The very decent Christiean human observation lies in the suggestion that a world-weary gigolo may come to feel disgusted with himself for exploiting unhappy women, and a professional vamp may be a very respectable girl earning her own and her family's support. Two stories originally created for Hercule Poirot were subsequently transferred to the more appropriate Parker Pyne.

But the last six Parker Pyne stories might equally have been transferred to Poirot. Mr Parker Pyne travels across the Middle East, going to several places Poirot or later thriller heroines would visit – the Stamboul train, Petra, Shiraz, Baghdad, the Nile, Delphi – and straightforwardly solving mysteries there. In these stories, Agatha mastered the art of sketching in an exotic background without letting it take over the tale. But she really didn't need Parker Pyne in the role of detective. With a completely different plot, Poirot even inherited one of Parker Pyne's titles unchanged: "Death on the Nile".

He also silently inherited Mr Parker Pyne's efficient secretary Miss Lemon. *And* his associate Mrs Ariadne Oliver. But she merits personal and separate treatment.

MR PARKER PYNE: HERO OF A COLLECTION OF SHORT STORIES.

Mrs Ariadne Oliver

Perhaps Agatha Christie's most delightful creation, Mrs Oliver was introduced in the most perfunctory manner in the Parker Pyne story "The Case of the Discontented Soldier". A "sensational novelist" with 46 best-sellers to her credit, translated into seven languages including Hungarian, Japanese, Finnish and Abyssinian, Mrs Oliver works, surrounded by untidy sheets of manuscript and a bag of apples, in a room two floors above his office. She plots the adventures he stage manages for clients whose unhappiness stems from boredom. We are told nothing about her appearance. But her untidy work methods and passion for apples were Agatha's. And the plot that brings Major Wilbraham and Freda Clegg together includes the kidnapping that always featured in Agatha's thrillers and uses a phonograph record, as she had once used a dictaphone to create an alibi. Although Parker Pyne sets up another adventure much like an Agatha thriller in "The Case of the City Clerk", we are not told that Mrs Oliver played any part in its invention, and she might easily have disappeared without trace.

Instead she was reintroduced in *Cards on the Table* (1936) to join Poirot, Colonel Race and Superintendent Battle as the four detectives who must decide which of four suspects murdered their host in their presence at a bridge party. Mrs Oliver, relying on "woman's intuition", provides comic relief. She is not at this stage an obvious self-portrait of Agatha. She lives in a Harley Street flat, and works in a room hideously decorated with a wallpaper of jungle birds. She has a loud bass voice – Agatha had a soft soprano – and rushes intrusively into any conversation with her opinions. She experiments with unsuitable styles for her untidy grey hair. She is a big woman who has some difficulty getting in and out of her little car. She is heavy enough to have suffered several inconvenient accidents with flimsy garden furniture. She is a self-declared feminist, constantly wishing that a woman might be appointed head of Scotland Yard and objecting to "those dreadful women police in funny hats who bother people in the parks". Indeed, policewomen's hats were hideous in the interwar period, and the middle classes were obsessed with the erroneous belief that gentlemen arrested for public indecency or drunkenness in Hyde Park were being framed.

TWO FINE NOVELS FEATURING MRS OLIVER.

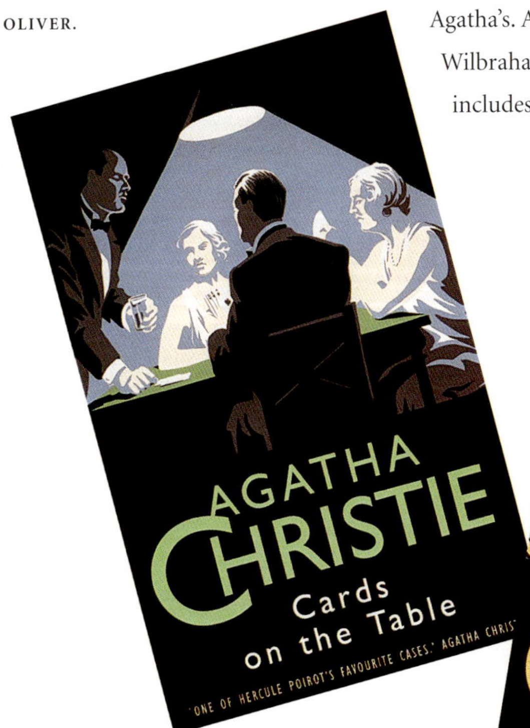

Only her rather untidily handsome appearance with "substantial shoulders" – often a Victorian euphemism for the bust – her constant clutter of books, papers and apples, and her comments on the craft of writing link her clearly to her creator. And the comments are extremely interesting.

Mrs Oliver admires a reader who spots the use of identical plot structure in wildly different situations: a murder on a rubber plantation in one book, the theft of Cabinet papers in another. But in each case the plot turns on the victim's having arranged the crime. So, like Agatha, Mrs Oliver cares first and foremost about the well-planned trick plot.

By contrast she couldn't care less about accuracy in detail: the precise ranks of police officers or the ways in which crimes are really investigated. Her readers want death, suspense and mystery, not a documentary on police procedure. If the newspapers can get things wrong, so can Mrs Oliver.

And Mrs Christie. Whose carelessness in this case casually reduces Mrs Oliver's 46 best sellers to 32.

But the true fascination of Ariadne Oliver was her revelation of Agatha's feelings about her detective hero. Mrs Oliver has created a Finnish detective, and is "always getting letters from Finland pointing out something impossible that he's said or done." No one has ever doubted that this is the voice of Agatha, regretting having made Poirot Belgian.

Sixteen years later, Mrs Oliver was revived in *Mrs McGinty's Dead.* And by now there could be no mistaking the self-caricature. The Finnish detective is named as Sven Hjerson, and provokes a positive wail as Mrs Oliver declares herself tired of his vegetarianism and his mannerisms. But she also protests about dramatizers and film-makers who want to change his character radically, and make him a younger man to meet an inappropriate love interest. She complains about the iniquitous tax situation that means the more she writes the more money she loses. With a slight increase in scattiness (probably reflecting Max's affectionate view of Agatha's untidiness) Mrs Oliver had become an undisguised self-caricature, walking round her room mouthing dialogue to herself and pulling at her hair when she composed.

AGATHA, THE MODEL FOR MRS ARIADNE OLIVER.

Nor was the caricature restricted to words. The Agatha who created Ariadne Oliver in the 1930s was a handsome middle-aged woman with a large frame. The Agatha who revived her in the 1950s was, frankly, a fat lady with grossly swollen ankles. There was comfort in laughing at her size as the slightly younger edition of herself "bulges"out of sight or munches a Bath bun to compensate for a light breakfast.

And in the last decade of Agatha's writing career, Mrs Oliver came into her own as Poirot's one real friend since Hastings. There was good reason for this. Uniquely among Mrs Christie's middle-aged and elderly detectives, Mrs Oliver was lovable. In *Cards on the Table* she burst into tears on discovering a murder. Nothing could have been more unlike that other elderly lady created in the 1930s, Miss Jane Marple.

Miss Marple

Miss Marple appeared to the world in 1930 in *The Murder at the Vicarage.* "A white-haired old lady with a gentle, appealing manner", according to vicar Len Clement. "The worst cat in the village", according to his wife. It seems an appropriate description.

She is at the centre of a group of prurient, nosey old women whose hobby is malicious gossip. The others are openly vinegary. Miss Marple's gentle and slightly twittery manner masks her steelier and more accurate observation. Her hobbies of gardening and bird-watching mask her real dedication to snooping on her neighbours, masked under the description of "studying human nature". Her garden is a vantage point from which, under the pretext of weeding, she can keep an eye on the comings and goings in the high street. Her bird-watching binoculars are often turned to observing the activities of featherless bipeds. Agatha's own genuine nice-mindedness prevented her from sensing the alarming overtones of the Peeping Tom, which were certainly unintended.

JOAN HICKMAN AS MISS MARPLE IN *THE BODY IN THE LIBRARY.*

And yet, by the end of the book, the Reverend Len can conclude that, "Really Miss Marple is rather a dear ..." And over another 10 novels and a raft of short stories, this benign aspect of Miss Marple increasingly took over, making her ultimately as popular a detective protagonist as Hercule Poirot, although he appears in three times as many books. The nauseating sobriquet "a fluffy old pussy" is constantly attached to her, and she seems an icon of comfortable English Heritage village life.

Her English country village is superbly vaguely somewhere in England. St Mary Mead is said to be in Kent; in "Downshire"; somewhere accessible by a train heading west from Paddington ... At times it really seems to be in Devon. St Mary Mead, and its attendant town Market Basing, in fact, fly around southern England as restlessly as the Holy House of Loreto.

From the outset, Miss Marple was equipped with adjuncts which gave her a recognizable voice and firmly identifiable character. Her nephew Raymond West writes modern poetry with no capital letters and modern novels which Miss Marple feels concern remarkably

AUNTIE-GRANNIE TAKING THE AIR IN TORQUAY.

unpleasant people. There was only one serious poet who consistently wrote in lower case, though ee cummings's instantly identifiable verse was parodied in Don Marquis's *archy and mehitabel.* Setting aside his typography, Cummings was an easily accessible and charming lyric poet whom Agatha, an admirer of T.S. Eliot, would have had no difficulty appreciating. But Miss Marple cheerfully appeals to that great middle-class Philistine audience which that modern art was ramp and modern poetry was incomprehensible and modern novels were disgusting.

Few of Agatha Christie's readers would have suspected that she did not share these views, though they might have observed that Miss Marple is given lightly comic treatment as she voices her critical opinions of Raymond's tastes. And the sheathing of the cat's claws is evident from the outset when Raymond is mentioned. He is richer than Miss Marple and generous to her, and she really appreciates this.

Quasi-prudish spinsterliness is Miss Marple's other defining characteristic. She blushes slightly on hinting at pregnancy. She speaks of "gentlemen" as though they were a different and dangerous species. Yet at heart Miss Marple is unshockable. She is neither surprised nor disgusted by premarital sex or the promiscuity of some young women. She does not approve of adultery, but does not think it defines the adulterer's moral status. She is quite unperturbed if a young woman's adolescent crush on an older lesbian arouses the latter's intense passion. She does not approve of that passion leading to murder. She is not appalled by a doctor's suffering an unconsummated incestuous passion for his sister. She is concerned that it leads him to jealous murder. Unlike the D.H. Lawrence of *The Fox* or the Thomas Hardy of *Tess of the D'Urbervilles,* she does not imagine that true and natural love justifies killing a perverse impediment. Mrs Christie's sound moral sense keeps her "sensational fiction" in a balance appropriate to its setting.

Miss Marple's detective powers are less happily created than Poirot's, however. Her reiterated habit of seeing the similarity between great crimes and the little peccadilloes she remembers from village society is manifestly borrowed from Fr Brown, and doesn't really convince. Her uncritical tendency to believe the worst of other people, derived from Auntie-Grannie, doesn't really add up to percipience. Although she may observe and deduce brilliantly –as she does in *The Body in the Library* – she is equally likely to jump to some unexplained conclusion which turns out to be right. Her gardening may explain her ability to see landscape alterations concealing past murder victims' buried bodies. But if her insight really showed her the truth at an early stage of

MARGARET RUTHERFORD AS MISS MARPLE IN *MURDER MOST FOUL.*

Sleeping Murder, why did she allow another victim to die? If her permitted "one coincidence" had not taken place in *The Murder at the Vicarage,* how could there ever have been a murder at all? The success of the character rests on the paradox of her unlikelihood as a fine detective. The best Miss Marple books are as ingeniously plotted as almost any Agatha wrote. But the true detective, following the clues and hopefully coming to the right conclusion, is usually the reader rather than the heroine.

Truth and Fiction

THE YOUNG DAVID LLOYD GEORGE: AGATHA'S "MISSING PRIME MINISTER."

Very early in her career, Agatha obliged Major Belcher by making him Sir Eustace Pedler in *The Man in the Brown Suit.* She was amusing herself when she made Belcher's immensely respectable secretary Bates – with his face like a poisoner – into Pedler's secretary. She would amuse herself again, 12 years later, when *Murder in Mesopotamia* sketched the Woolleys' archaeological team, with an almost invisible bit-part for Max as the sensible young man Emmott, and a centre-stage depiction of Katharine Woolley which the Mallowans feared might have been too recognizable. Agatha did not make a practice of modelling villains or thankfully dispatched victims on her acquaintances, though the American monologue actress Ruth Draper could hardly have objected to the admiring portrait of her performances given by a virtuous victim in *Lord Edgware Dies.*

Agatha did consistently use places and plays she knew. Gielgud's performance in *The Duchess of Malfi* is specified in *Sleeping Murder,* and Miss Marple also likes the opera and enjoyed most of J.M. Barrie's plays (except *Quality Street*). We have seen that both Parker Pyne and Poirot trail Agatha on the Orient Express and around the Middle East. She was tactful and professional in her use of exotic places. Her mysteries were not held up by lengthy descriptions of Abu Simbel or Petra, indeed the latter was very economically sketched, both the story "The Pearl of Price" and the novel *Appointment with Death* suggesting that Agatha was less impressed by the amazing "rose-red" cave and tomb fronts and porticoes than by the sacrificial mound behind the city and the hidden gully leading into it.

Politics and politicians were something of a problem for an "apolitical" thriller-writer. David Lloyd George might have modelled as "The Missing Prime Minister", but the short-lived Canadian-born Conservative Andrew Bonar Law seems more likely as the "colourless" premier of *The Secret Adversary.* One of the leading suspects, Sir James Edgerton KC, with his handsome features, winning personality and seat in Parliament, could not be written off as a mere stock character in the generation that knew Marshall Hall.

The interesting *Labours of Hercules* story "The Augean Stables" anticipates gutter-press news-gathering that would give more prominence to silly sex scandals than to actual political defalcations. The rock-solid traditionalist politicians at the centre are manifestly Conservatives, although they head "the People's Party". Their revered ex-leader "Honest John" Hammett suggests Baldwin, and recognizing this, Agatha is careful to make authorial mention of Baldwin's pipe and Chamberlain's umbrella, to make it quite clear she intends no reflection on these ex-premiers. Stephen Faraday, a stuffed-shirt Conservative MP whose career is forwarded by his aristocratic Old High Tory wife in *Sparkling Cyanide*, strongly suggests the way dull reactionary Conservatives saw the liberal-minded intellectual Harold Macmillan at the time it was written in 1945.

But what was Agatha doing when she named the flamboyant diplomat-hero of *Passenger to Frankfurt* Sir Stafford Nye? The names inevitably suggest Attlee's austere chancellor Sir Stafford Cripps and radical rebel minister of health and housing, Nye Bevan. Yet this is one of her most determined right-of-centre protests against young leftist demonstrators of the 1960s. The throwaway phrase, "Petronella will be there", is an affectionate glance at Vanessa Redgrave, whose slightly unusual forename used on its own easily identified the most prominent member of the Socialist Workers' Party at demos.

Agatha glanced at familiar true crimes occasionally. Crippen is mentioned a couple of times, though he is given an unhistorical "boastful personality" in *Three Act Tragedy*, a novel which also turns Elizabeth MacKintosh, doubly *nom de plume*-d as detective novelist (Josephine Tey) and playwright (Gordon Daviot) into Muriel Wills, who writes plays under the masculine name Anthony Aston. And an aside glances at the comic figure of Harold Williamson, Rector of Stiffkey, defrocked for associating with very young prostitutes before pretending to fast in a barrel to "prove" his innocence. *Mrs McGinty's Dead* turns on a past murder which is transparently Crippen's. But still more remarkably Agatha called the remembered Crippen character Craig and a nerdy suspect Bentley, just before the murder of PC Miles etched those names into the annals of crime. The racing driver who handles getaway cars in *At Bertram's Hotel* may have been suggested by Roy John James of the Great Train Robbery.

There are memories of henpecked Major Armstrong who poisoned his wife; of Lizzie Borden, the spinster axe murderer, and of Mrs Hearne, accused of serving poisoned salmon paste sandwiches. And names seem to have stuck in Mrs Christie's mind. Miss Tommy Tucker of Newfoundland was murdered by young people she had befriended in 1950. Eleven years later Thomasina Tucker was poisoned in Agatha's *The Pale Horse*. Centenarian provincial actress Mrs Helen Cresswell told the press she would love to read *Lady Audley's Secret* again in 1945, and received six sackfuls from a sympathetic public. 12 years later in *Greenshaw's Folly*, retired provincial actress Mrs Cresswell committed murder over a will hidden in the same book. But these seem to be unconscious recollections and associations. Agatha Christie never really wrote *roman à clef*.

THE HANGING OF DR CRIPPEN.

"VANESSA WAS THERE": VANESSA REDGRAVE WITH TARIQ ALI AT A 1960S DEMO.

The Golden Age

"THE TREASURY" PORTICO AT PETRA.

The golden age of the traditional detective novel is conventionally fixed as the 1920s and 1930s. The golden age of Agatha Christie is probably best placed at circa 1934 to 1944. She had written first-class whodunnits in the previous years, *Lord Edgware Dies* and *The Sittaford Mystery*, for example. She would write more in the succeeding years, including *The Hollow* and *The Crooked House*. But between 1934 and 1944 she sent Hercule Poirot on those travels through the Middle East from the Orient Express to Cairo, which had already been followed by Mr Parker Pyne.

Her wartime thriller, *N or M*, was much better organized than its predecessors. She perfected her lateral-thinking sleight of hand that led the reader to look in completely the wrong direction. *Death in the Clouds* misdirects us because we cannot believe that anyone truly loving and loved by a lead character with a trustworthy point of view could be the murderer. *The Body in the Library* is not what we imagine and its discovery in the library doesn't have the significance we expect. *Murder on the Nile* exploits and improves the two tricks which had made *Styles* such a successful first novel. And two more great classics of lateral thinking: *Murder on the Orient Express* (1934) and *And Then There Were None* (1939: originally titled *Ten Little Niggers* or in America *Ten Little Indians*) sealed her reputation as the greatest of all whodunnit writers.

If you have not read these books and wish to do so without knowing the solutions, turn the page at once.

Fame, of course, reaped criticism. No writer, not even Shakespeare, escapes the thumbs down from some reader somewhere. Edmund Wilson took *Roger Ackroyd* as the exemplary instance of a boring book in a pointless form. Raymond Chandler, memorably countered the admiring opinion that the keenest brain could not have solved *Murder on the Orient Express* with the view that only an idiot could have imagined all the passengers in a *wagon lit* carriage combining to kill a common enemy leaving clues which deliberately incriminated separate individuals.

And Then There Were None is an even more impressive instance of Agatha's ability to create suspense. I knew that all the people on the island died, and which of them was responsible before I read it. But it remains a page-turner that I can return to with pleasure in the masterly way it is built up and carried forward.

Not that Agatha's notorious inaccuracies and willingness to exploit hunches and coincidence were corrected in these masterpieces. She was herself embarrassed at having failed to discover the inordinate length of South American blowpipes before hiding one on the plane in *Death in the Clouds*. Poirot's laborious interviews simply don't suggest any way in which some of the Orient Express travellers might be connected with the Armstrong murder. His conclusion is something of a hunch. *And Then There Were None* holds the reader's attention by following the nursery rhyme's pattern which seems to make clear how the next murder is to be accomplished. A moment's reflection shows how lucky the murderer was that – to take one example – Rogers the butler happened to chop firewood in the early morning, permitting him to follow the nursery rhyme which had the fourth little boy chop himself in half while chopping up sticks. The argument that a sadistically inclined little boy with a strong sense of fair play would inevitably become a hanging judge is very dubious psychology.

The rhyme itself is an obvious instance of Agatha's long-running pleasure in basing plots or titles on nursery rhymes or children's chanting games ("Goosey Goosey Gander" in *N or M*; "Three Blind Mice" in *The Mousetrap*; "This Little Piggy Went to Market" in *Five Little Pigs*; "Sing a Song of Sixpence" in a couple of short stories as well as *A Pocket Full of Rye*). They had a huge advantage that they would be instantly recognized by all her readers, whereas the poems and literary quotations she also used – *The Hollow*, *The Postern of Fate*, *The Mirror Crack'd from Side to Side*, *By the Pricking of my Thumbs* – had to be spelled out, or, as in the last case, glossed over with a pretence that she didn't really remember where it came from.

BURGH ISLAND: SETTING FOR *AND THEN THERE WERE NONE* AND *EVIL UNDER THE SUN*.

It was bad luck that the rhyme "Ten Little Niggers" was about to be consigned to oblivion for its political incorrectness. Christie's more sensitive American publishers instantly renamed what is arguably Agatha's greatest or most memorable achievement as the irrelevant counting game "Ten Little Indians". A lady of Agatha's generation probably didn't normally refer to individual people as niggers. – Mrs Ariadne Oliver, inventing a rubbishy racist plot for Mr Parker Pyne, refers to the two black actors employed as "darkies", and the narrative calls them Negroes with a capital N. But even liberal internationalist ladies dyed their faded cardigans "nigger" brown and referred to "nigger" minstrels on the pier without a qualm. Conservatives such as Agatha might easily have thought and spoken of rebellious colonial "subject races" as niggers. And crude racist insensitivity really was Agatha's Achilles' heel. It tripped her up uncomfortably in the immediate post-war period.

"SING A SONG OF SIXPENCE" – THE NURSERY RHYME AGATHA QUOTED IN THREE TITLES.

Rivals

DOROTHY L. SAYERS: "CONTRARY TO POPULAR OPINION I AM NOT A MAN."

Agatha was too much of a lady to think competitively about heading the new mistresses of crime fiction. But from the standpoint of many critical observers, she had no sooner made her name than a rival eclipsed her. Dorothy L. Sayers produced *Whose Body?* in 1923, and her detective hero Lord Peter Wimsey quickly captivated a readership that might otherwise have admired Agatha's more restrained young modernity. Wimsey owed much to the American writer S.S. Van Dine's detective Philo Vance, an upper class know-all with an affected manner of speech. Agatha wisely did not up the ante by going any further than she had already done with Tommy and Tuppence's slangy "bright young thinginess".

But Wimsey was said to be modelled on Roy Ridley, the dashing and debonair chaplain and English tutor of Balliol. Dorothy Sayers was an Oxford graduate and had no intention of letting anyone forget it. Wimsey had a Balliol man's "effortless superiority", excelling as cricketer, scholar, fast driver and connoisseur. Only none of these things were perfectly demonstrated. His scholarship was announced but not proved. His taste was shaky. The novels did not suggest that Miss Sayers knew anything much about cricket.

What's more, Wimsey was not really convincing as a duke's younger brother. Like Archie Christie, Roy Ridley was an Old Cliftonian, and it may have been evident to Agatha that Lord Peter was not really the super-pukka sahib he was supposed to suggest.

But he was entertaining in his own right for those who enjoyed a flow of "ironic" banter in upper class twitspeak. And at times Dorothy Sayers created a background that justifiably held the reader. She really knew about advertising agencies, having worked in one. And her knowledge gave genuine strength to *Murder Must Advertise*. She was a Lincolnshire vicar's daughter and her creation of a church bell-ringing community in Lincolnshire made *The Nine Taylors* a favourite detective novel for readers who were not inspired to groan at Lord Peter's revealing himself as an unsuspected master of change-ringing. It may well have been the influence of Dorothy Sayers' popularity that encouraged Agatha to give decisive backgrounds drawn from her own travel experiences to so many of the books of her own golden age in the 1930s. She was not tempted to follow Miss Sayers in claiming that her books were "comedies of manners" and criticizing the public for failing to appreciate them.

Ngaio Marsh, the New Zealand creator of Superintendent Roderick Alleyne, drew from Agatha the perception that an excellent mystery arose from proposing that the obvious suspect simply couldn't have done it, and then showing just how they had. It led her to some complicated and elaborate murder methods, something on which many golden age writers plumed themselves, but which Agatha rarely imitated. Her knowledge of poisons made her in fact a better creator of convincingly mysterious murder methods than her rivals. Her use of the elaborately planned alibi like a booby-trap in *Hercule Poirot's Christmas* comes as an interesting response to the request for a murder with "lots of blood". And the blood in fact is part of the trick rather than gruesome gore for its own sake.

Ngaio Marsh also specialized in the long sequence of interviews in which Alleyne takes the story of one witness or suspect after another until, from their combined tales, the lies and red herrings can be eliminated and the truth deduced. Here again, Agatha occasionally used the method. But characteristically, in *Murder on the Orient Express*, the interviews don't eliminate red herrings and narrow down the search to the one inevitable suspect. Though the reader is tricked into believing they must be doing so.

The third new mistress of crime was Margery Allingham. Her detective was as aristocratic as Wimsey, though less obtrusively and foppishly so. And, like Wimsey and Alleyne, "Albert Campion" was young enough to fall in love, marry and grow older with his creator and her readers. Agatha's preference for detectives with the wisdom of age precluded her from doing this with any protagonists except Tommy and Tuppence.

The postwar Allingham received critical acclaim when, in *Tiger in the Smoke*, she expressed the anxieties of a generation which felt that the amorality of urban youths trained in violence by the war was leading to materialist moral anarchy. With a gentle and saintly canon of the Church of England in the background and a completely up-to-date young villain in Jack Havoc, Allingham seemed to have realized the dream of making the popular detective novel or thriller into a work as serious as Graham Greene's best "entertainments". Only the climactic over-romantic idea of a hidden treasure lowered the book clearly to the realm of popular fiction. This may have inspired Agatha to attempt her most ambitiously profound whodunnit suspenser *Endless Night*.

AGATHA AND NGAIO MARSH.

Like Allingham, she ended her book with a bit of a scramble conforming to her basic genre. Like Allingham, she rather left the impression that the upper classes have an inside track to virtue. And Margery Allingham certainly showed that, unlike Mrs Christie, she could portray the underside of London. But in her protagonist, Agatha came far closer than Margery Allingham to creating moral tragedy. It was not something she needed to attempt again in detective fiction. She wrote as Mary Westmacott if she felt she had, in the most serious sense, "something to say".

Romances

ROMANTIC FICTION
OF THE 1920S AND 1930S.

The novels Agatha wrote under the *nom de plume* Mary Westmacott are often described as romantic fiction. This is misleading. Several of them simply do not turn on romantic love at all in the usual sense. Other serious concerns, far beyond an Ethel M. Dell or a Barbara Cartland, frequently lie at their heart. Yet there was a trace of the popular romantic fiction writer to be found in Agatha's work, especially the light-hearted variety represented in Jean Morton's *Daddy-Long-Legs.*

Not that there was anything light-hearted about that extraordinary first venture into romantic fiction, *Magnolia Blossom.* And the 1929 story *Next to a Dog* also carried a slightly acrid flavour. The war-widowed heroine is genteelly but literally starving herself to death rather than accept a residential teaching or caring post which would separate her from the dog which was given her by her husband. As in *Magnolia Blossom,* there is a distinct hint that marriage for money or security is prostitution, though in this case there is complete sympathy for the heroine as she nearly accepts the proposal of a man who sadistically enjoys her distaste for his kisses. While all comes well in the end when a kindly old dog-loving gentleman offers her a post where the dog can accompany her – and we anticipate wedding bells as she recovers from her bereaved grief – the original predicament is strongly realized and points to Agatha's unusually hard-centred perception of sex and love.

Hard-centred, that is, by the standard one might expect from the creator of Mr Harley Quin, the lover's friend, and the clutch of light-hearted romantic stories Agatha wrote in the 1930s. *The Listerdale Mystery* is almost a wish-fulfilment fantasy for Clara Miller. A ladylike widow in reduced circumstances is rented a perfect Queen Anne residence for a ridiculously low sum. It transpires that this is the doing of eccentric Lord Listerdale, who compensates for his misspent youth by making beautiful properties available to distressed gentlefolk. And naturally, he falls in love with our heroine. She, meanwhile, has enjoyed the advantage of a decent base for her daughter's coming-out season and surroundings which persuade her son that his growing attachment to a low class tobacconist's assistant is misplaced. Mills and Boon never issued a more exemplary mixture of snobbery and misty moonlight love – though Mills and Boon might have recognized that their readership included sufficient tobacconists' assistants to make a little more tact desirable.

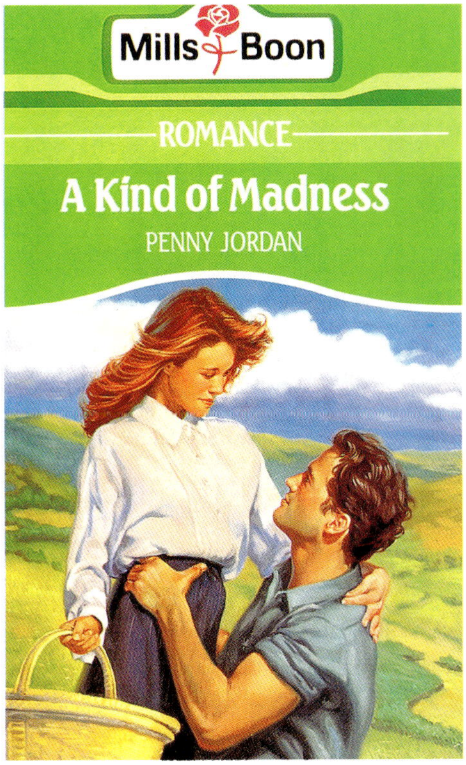

ROMANTIC FICTION TODAY.

A couple of stories show Agatha venturing into this unfamiliar lower class territory. She evidently feels that cars are or should be rather out of the reach of petty pen-pushers. O. Henry would have exulted in the would-be swell young clerk taking his shop assistant girlfriend out for a spin like the nobs. And he would have made it seem appropriate. Agatha thinks it almost comically inappropriate. A young man wins enough in a newspaper competition to buy a smart car, though he knows his prudent fiancée would prefer the money to go into a nest egg for a house. When he enjoys a splendidly improbable adventure with some "bright young things" who mistake him for the kind of real professional jewel thief they are sportingly imitating, he gains the courage to override his young lady's caution, sweep her up in his arms and tell her they will not wait any longer to get married. Agatha's love of daring and risk-taking are well to the fore, but coming from the real life background in which Monty Miller could pile failing venture on failing venture until retiring to sponge off his sisters, she was not really offering the wisest counsel to young people who had no wealthy relatives and no resources but what their menial work earned them.

With folk more of her own class, she still seems to associate romance with mildly dashing bounders like Monty rather than hard-working subordinates like Max. She writes two stories about young men whose idleness around the office leads them to accept with insouciance the well-earned sack and proceed to sudden adventures which win them both girl and fortune. A young man whose girlfriend snobbishly abandons him for wealthier and more glamorous company at an English seaside town makes his fortune by saving *The Rajah's Emerald* when he naughtily uses a private bathing hut, and accidentally comes away with the wrong pair of trousers. These are light-hearted tales, and the jocular teasing courtship Agatha approves in her own class was reflected in the heroes and heroines of some of her novels.

Perhaps the extreme example is Jerry Burton, narrator of *The Moving Finger*, who persistently addresses the girl he is falling in love with as "Funnyface" or "Slabface". At first glance this seems a glaring example of that unromantic English conduct which supposedly makes English women easy prey for Continental gigolos. On the other hand, it obviously appealed to Agatha far more than the uncomfortable stiff-collared courtesies of lower-middle class suitors, and probably derived from the "kind of merry war" which makes Beatrice and Benedick of Shakespeare's *Much Ado About Nothing* more satisfactory lovers than Romeo and Juliet in many ways.

Mary Westmacott

The six Mary Westmacott novels can easily be underrated. Although their plots may be melodramatic and the complications and frustrations of love are always featured, they are not, in the cheap sense, "romantic novels" as they are too often described.

On the other hand, they can easily be overrated. A concentration on the themes that interested Agatha shows her mind to be deep and serious. She was a mistress of pace; a mistress of convincing and character-revealing dialogue. These virtues may mask her extravagant plotting and scrambles to a finish, habits formed in detective fiction. Nor does her characterization usually have solid depth. She sketches highlights and lowlights of personality to illustrate the moral or psychological topic engrossing her. So her novels become discussion pieces without, in the end, illuminating us about types of persons we had not known before. And the discussions are the work of a thoroughly decent, homespun moralist rather than of an intellectual with an interest in moral philosophy.

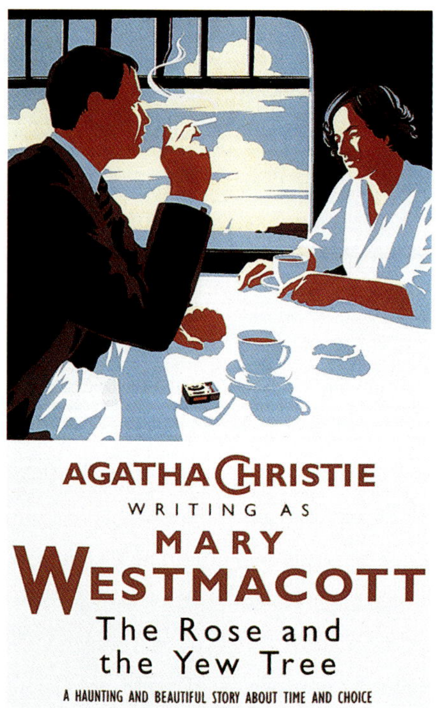

AGATHA'S MOST AMBITIOUS SERIOUS NOVEL *THE ROSE AND THE YEW TREE.*

Not, I hasten to say, that this is a fault. Graham Greene's early studies of tortured souls are in no way improved by the overlay of unquestioned theology which sits heavily on the shoulders of a Brighton mobster and his waitress girlfriend, or unbalances the conflict of ideals between the whisky priest and the atheist lieutenant. It is with other writers of plainly observed psychology and morality in realistic well-paced narratives – the Arnot Robertsons (*Ordinary Families*) or James Kennaways (*Tunes of Glory*) – that Mary Westmacott must be measured and found wanting.

Giant's Bread, the first Mary Westmacott novel, has far too many protagonists with their stories woven together as if a wide range of suspects was needed. A tangle of motives drives the plot forward: the wish to retain an old family home (a frequent theme of Agatha's); different drives to create or encourage new music; conflicting and unrecognized romantic and erotic urges; a rather preposterous catastrophe in which the hero makes a choice he later realizes to have been wrong. Yet these complicated themes are so inherently interesting that Agatha's excellent biographer, Janet Morgan, discusses the book favourably for several sentences before remarking, as if surprised by the fact, that "the plot is, on reflection, daft."

Unfinished Portrait is a predictable autobiographical novel. Pseudonymous authorship allowed Agatha to give free rein to her anger over her marital breakdown and examine her complicated love for Clara. She could be livelier and cheekier about the also-ran men with whom she had flirted than she was in open autobiography. But, as wise commentators have cautioned, although Max said this was her best self-portrait, the mistress of self-condemnatory dialogue should not be trusted entirely when Archie's fictional counterpart is coldly insensitive about other people's suffering, or brutally tells Agatha's counterpart that his love for her will not survive her youthful good looks.

A Daughter's a Daughter was first written as a play in the 1930s, and only later turned into a novel. Despite its date of publication (1930), its theme of possessive love in the daughter-mother relationship was typical of the personal matter in the pre-war Westmacott novels.

The last three Mary Westmacotts expose the deep concerns of the mature Agatha Christie. All three turn on religious conversion experiences and show that Agatha took a rationally mystical christianity very seriously indeed, even if she discreetly preferred not to wear her faith on her sleeve like Dorothy Sayers. Her profound sensitivity to the spiritual influence of the desert was allowed free play, as it could not be in detective novels where it would intrude on the plot. And repeatedly Agatha demonstrated her conviction that churchy insistence on chastity as essential virtue was not merely misplaced, it reversed spiritual truth. Truly spiritual characters would rejoice in their own sexuality; not lasciviously, not tartily, but with a quiet defiance that shocked and exposed the hollowness of the supposed good.

The Rose and the Yew Tree, its title taken from T.S. Eliot's *Little Gidding*, was her most ambitious book, and, like Graham Greene's *The End of the Affair* or John Irving's *Owen Meaney*, made a daring attempt to justify the miraculous ways of God to man in a rationalist materialist age. One can only applaud the wish to show how an almost perverse erotic love transforms a harsh go-getter into an active saint. One can only regret that the difficulty of portraying the spiritually pure though sexually active woman, whose influence converts the protagonist, leaves her mysteriously unrealized, despite the wise attempt to present her externally through others' eyes.

That compulsive act of artistic creativity, *Absent in the Spring*, led to the end of the Mary Westmacotts when the pseudonym was exposed in the Library of Congress catalogue. Since the story of a dreadful mammon of righteousness rejecting the truths she sees in the desert must have been provoked by someone Agatha knew, it is easy to see why she felt that she could not go on writing with such truth to her perceptions if her models might recognize themselves and suffer humiliation.

LEFT TO RIGHT: DOROTHY TUTIN, GRAHAM GREENE AND ERIC PORTMAN CONSIDER A PLAYSCRIPT. "MARY WESTMACOTT" SHARED GREENE'S UNORTHODOX RELIGIOUS DEDICATION AND CONVERSION WITHOUT COMMITMENT TO ORTHODOX THEOLOGY.

Keeping Up With The Young

THE BUBBLE CAR: A LATE 1950S INVENTION RAPIDLY SUPERSEDED BY THE MINI.

In her fifties, with a husband 14 years younger, Agatha had no difficulty in combining maturity with youth at heart. As she went on writing through her sixties and seventies, however, it became increasingly clear that keeping up with the times entailed a little effort. Tommy and Tuppence were always roughly Agatha's age and could be elderly with elderly folks' perception of the world around them without putting any strain on the narrative. But Poirot and Miss Marple had always felt older than the authorial narrative voice creating their adventures. And Agatha's books of the 1950s and '60s show her making conscious efforts to keep an eye on changing times so that her backgrounds and settings and younger characters continue to convince. A bubble car, for example, makes a random appearance in the 1958 novel *Ordeal By Innocence*, which would enable the social historian to date the book precisely if its publication history were somehow lost.

At Bertram's Hotel is a classic instance of the author in her seventies trying to show herself aware of the modern world and feel younger than Miss Marple, whose age, given in this book as 75, was in fact exactly Agatha's. The imaginative idea of a hotel which has perfectly preserved, yet slightly overdone the interwar atmosphere of discreet traditional luxury for retired admirals and elderly clerics and judges makes a deliberate contrast with the swinging sixties. Agatha never uses the term, and, indeed, the lubricious world of Stephen Ward and wife-swapping and recreational drugs would not have shocked or especially startled an old lady who had always known that such things went on and never mistook tasteless folly and self-indulgence for supreme wickedness. But she mentions the Beatles. She adroitly sends her elderly canon to lose himself on the way to a conference on the topically appropriate Dead Sea Scrolls. And as we have seen, she was probably aware that the Great Train Robbery had exposed a genuinely talented racing driver who handled cars for the mobs. The cool and entertaining amorality of her young protagonist Elvira's early jewel theft is akin to the cool and initially attractive presentation of trendy young crooks in the 1960s television serial "Big Breadwinner Hogg". That programme's controversial presentation of the kinds of genuine savage violence used by the London gangs of the time (notably the Krays and Richardsons) was not the kind of crime Agatha's escapist

STEPHEN WARD, SWINGER OF THE '60S UNDER ARREST.

puzzles ever delineated in detail. And so her casual acceptance that Elvira and her mother might share an erotic interest in the same dashing young man escaped the attention of the decade's moral censors, who continued fondly to imagine that dear safe old Agatha Christie's ethical standards were close to those of Mrs Mary Whitehouse.

But in the end, Agatha really was too old to run with the '60s pack. The Beatles, pop singers and "spivs" are linked as types of undesirable modernity that disgruntle the traditionalist patrons of Bertram's Hotel. But spivs, the black marketeering wide boys of rationing days, were no longer a part of the contemporary scene. It does not seem, in context, that Agatha was intentionally distancing herself from her elderly characters by giving them the older person's trait of using outdated slang.

And the use of the name Elvira for a young person born in the 1940s is another elderly author's mistake. After Mrs Elvira Barney narrowly escaped hanging for shooting her layabout lover in 1932, her distinctive forename practically vanished from the registers. Agatha managed to make an intended '60s trendy sound like a louche '30s "bright young thing".

Three years later, in *Hallowe'en Party*, she shows herself willing to accept that young people's outlandish fashions don't make them outlandishly inhuman. Two boys, aged 16 and 18 who alternate between extreme "mod" gear (pink and mauve velvet jackets with frilled shirts) and the all-black "rocker" alternative, are not, as we might anticipate, exemplars of the juvenile amorality which leads to blackmail and murder. They are extremely decent kids whom Poirot calls in to help him at the end.

In practice, the elderly Mrs Christie had always tried to keep a weather-eye open for the externals of young people's lives. *Third Girl* in 1966 showed her aware of the rooming habits of the young, and much better informed about the effects of marijuana than had been the case in 1947 when she wrote *The Flock of Geryon* and nursed the delusion that an injection of hashish would induce immediate erotic hallucinations and enslave the victim to the injector. *Hickory Dickory Dock* in 1955 showed her well aware of the internal appearance of an international student house and very familiar with the stereotypical differences between colonials: student Indians suspicious of black *confrères* and touchy about suspected slights from the English; Africans ebullient and outgoing; West Indians (in the days before independence, mass education and black consciousness had raised the profile of Europeanized Africans) were somewhat educationally superior. She also foresaw, prophetically, that drug-smugling was overtaking jewel-smuggling as a money-spinner for "mules".

Yet, as with the name Elvira, she retained some anachronistic linguistic habits from the 1930s. The Buchmanite anti-sexual evangelical movement had already started currying favour with anti-Communists and renamed itself Moral Rearmament in 1938. Agatha still thought of it under its pseudo-intellectual title, the Oxford Group.

FROM HOOLIGANS TO TEDDY BOYS: THE TWENTIETH CENTURY'S JUVENILE DELINQUENCY PROBLEM.

Hardening of The Arteries

Consider *The Pale Horse* (1961). One of Agatha's own favourites, and deservedly so. Few 71-year-old writers could ever have matched the ingenuity with which she invents an elaborate conspiracy to market contract killings without appearing to do so. (One wonders whether this was prompted by a semi-conscious wish to outdo Margery Allingham's brilliant conspiracy in *More Work for the Undertaker*, itself a remarkable elaboration and improvement on Conan Doyle's *The Disappearance of Lady Frances Carfax*). No other detective writer could have identified the mysterious symptoms of thallium poisoning, presenting genuine clues for the skilled toxicologist and a complete puzzle for anyone else. Few other writers could have created such successful suspense from witchcraft, *obeah* and psychic mumbo jumbo, while at the same time knowing a reader's flesh could be chilled without the author's committing to a belief in tosh.

A FILM ABOUT GRAHAME YOUNG – REAL LIFE MURDERER, WHO USED A RARE POISON NAMED IN *THE PALE HORSE*.

So how can I suggest that this remarkable work evinces a geriatric decline in old Mrs Christie's performance? Well, to start with the "detection" is thoroughly unsatisfactory. Poirot advises us to "trust no one" throughout the book. Yet there is no clue to suggest why he recognizes the murderer's incriminating statement as a complete pack of lies. And that unexplained hunch is all the detection he really does. The additional "psychological" insight that murderers are vain and always talk too much is one Agatha has used before. And it doesn't hold water as a generalization. One vaguely wonders which doctor or detective friend gave her this piece of misinformation to be trotted out when needed.

But worst of all is the accretion of missed and flubbed detail. The name Corrigan on an important list at the beginning of the book points to one of two characters. The clue is casually forgotten. John Despard suddenly becomes Hugh. Worst of all, Agatha's dual narrative technique slips in Chapter VI, when Mark Easterbrook is suddenly referred to in the third person while he is supposed to be narrating. The writer who had handled *The Five Little Pigs* narratives so competently would never have made such a mistake. (Nor can one compliment her copy editor for missing it).

Ten years later the anxieties of old age showed up pathetically as Agatha feared she must blame herself for the real life young murderer Grahame Young's use of thallium to start a mysterious epidemic at his workplace in Bovingdon. Young had been studying and experimenting with poisons all his life, spending most of his teens in secure custody after having killed his stepmother. The clever-dick killer who gave himself away by showing off his knowledge of thallium certainly didn't need a 10-year-old Christie book to teach him about it. And a younger Agatha would have robustly laughed off the silly press suggestion that her writing had taught Young how to kill.

But by the 1970s the signs of geriatric rambling were infecting most of her work. *Passenger to Frankfurt* (1970) comfortably takes the palm as her politically silliest book ever. Anti-Vietnam War demonstrations, Beatlemania, over-lenient court sentences, recreational drugs and sexual promiscuity are all supposed to be part of a Nazi youth revival, taking the anti-imperialist thinkers Fanon, Marcuse and Levi-Strauss as its gurus! An author's introduction suggests that this wild fantasy is a serious possibility. And for the only time in her life, Agatha sank to thinking that actively sexual young people were decadent.

The Miss Marple novel *Nemesis* the following year was filled with a good deal of vague meditation inside Miss Marple's head which didn't carry plot or characterization very far. The murder in the past which Miss Marple solves by the wildest of hunches is supposed to be one of a series of rape-murders. But the supposedly notorious series is completely forgotten as Miss Marple proves that a girl who was always believed to have been a runaway had actually been an unsuspected murder victim.

Elephants Can Remember (1972) allows Poirot and Mrs Oliver to hold endless desultory conversations about the forgetfulness of old age. Dull dialogue was now the easiest thing to write, it seems. The key to the mystery features two of Agatha's worst tried and trusted devices; identical twins to be confused with one another, and the "replacement" relative who lives unsuspected by her nearest and dearest for some time. Even Agatha's most impassioned admirers have found it impossible to give this book much praise, and it seems that favourable reviews were a courtesy to the 82-year-old national institution who somehow managed to keep churning out the Christie for Christmas.

Tommy and Tuppence's outing in *The Postern of Fate* the following year was the last of these. The old dears maunder on with inaccurate recollections. Agatha obviously wrote from memory as they uncover a treasure trove of books they loved in childhood, including one called *The Psamayad*. She had forgotten that E Nesbit's masterpiece is called *Five Children and It*, and the sand fairy was a "psammead". Clues are set up and forgotten. Another silly political conspiracy lies behind the book. And the relatively obscure line of James Elroy Flecker supplying the title would support those who wrongly assumed Agatha's tastes to be hopelessly middlebrow.

BEATLEMANIA: MASS HYSTERIA THAT AGATHA FEARED MIGHT MEAN A RESURGENCE OF FASCISM.

Solving 'em

ALBERT FINNEY AS POIROT IN THE MOVIE VERSION OF *MURDER ON THE ORIENT EXPRESS.*

It *can* be done. Remember you're not using a factual report to identify a murderer's giveaway mistakes, you're pitting your wits against a clever writer who tries to deceive you in such a way that when you are tricked you will be delighted and amused by the wit and cunning of her deception. But bear the following rules in mind, and you should solve three out of five of Agatha Christie's best whodunnits.

1. Somebody has an excellent motive. But he or she is so firmly ruled out by lack of means or opportunity that the detective or the police confidently cross them off the list of suspects from an early stage. *Suspect that person.* Can you work out a howdunnit to support the whodunnit? If the suspect really couldn't have committed the murderous act by any ingenious sleight of hand or preplanned booby trap, then look for a secret accomplice.

2. Don't give yourself a headache trying to answer the questions the detective says are important. They are not intended to help you, but to mislead you into worrying about minor details while innocently pointing you just a couple of compass points off the central truth. Don't worry too much about that favourite Agatha mystery clue, "What did X see over Y's shoulder behind Y's back that made X start just before the murder?" It may well mean that X or Y were implicated. But what was actually seen, or not seen, will often prove tangential, undeducible and unguessable. It's Agatha the conjuror directing your attention away from the real mechanism of the trick.

3. More people than the murderer may have guilty secrets. A shifty background character may be an embezzler or a thief quite unconnected with the murder. In a series of murders there may even be two quite different killers with different motives who accidentally and unwittingly alibi each other.

4. And in a sequence of murders, getting rid of a confederate or an unwitting witness to some giveaway action may be the motive for an apparently pointless killing.

5. Do look for tiny throwaway details in the lead-up to the crime. Re-read everything that tells you who was on the spot and who slipped out of the room for a good reason for a few minutes and who was thought to be safely asleep somewhere in the vicinity. Be especially suspicious if a tiny window of opportunity is never mentioned again.

5. Always be prepared for disguise and imposture. In the world of Agatha Christie, disguise can be so perfect that nobody recognizes a killer who suddenly reappears in a different persona, even if they were talking to them in their normal character a few minutes earlier and have known them all their lives. Impostors may have maintained a false identity for years to conceal a murder in the past, and nobody has suspected them. Identical twins are a cheap shot Agatha uses two or three times to make alibis or impostures perfect.

6. Remember that a really good murderer may allay suspicion by faking an attempt on his or her own life. And that the murderer definitely, any other witness possibly, *tells lies*.

7. Be prepared for the *Valley of Fear* trick. If the body isn't who everyone thinks it is, then an awful lot of calculation based on the victim's known movements is leading you up the garden path.

8. Enjoy to the maximum Agatha's craft with words. Bear in mind that names like Joyce and Hilary may identify a man or a woman, and Agatha will happily set her whole pack of characters (and you) looking for someone of the wrong gender. Think of contexts in which a scrap of paper reading, "I am possessed" would have nothing to do with an invasion by the devil. Exult in the cleverness which makes the eponymous (and tangential) clue *Why Didn't They Ask Evans?* mean something you could never have predicted.

9. And finally, the trick that made Agatha the Queen of Crime. She not only cheerfully stands every *literary* convention of character on its head, she uses them against you by making you believe they still apply. Notoriously, she is willing to say that the sympathetic narrator may be the murderer, provided he silently omits a number of his thoughts and actions until the denouement. A real or intended victim may be the murderer. A 'Watson' may be the murderer. The client asking for the investigation may be the murderer. A stolid investigating policeman may be the murderer. *All* the characters may have colluded in the murder. Thus far, usually innocent characters from the stock plot of the whodunnit.

But still more misleading, the juvenile lead 'hero' or "heroine" may be the murderer. The lover's eye giving us our point of view may be deceived. And so will we be if, as is the case in most popular fiction, we trust the heroine's hormones to identify a good guy for us. A handsome and charming man who is genuinely in love may still murder for pre-planned gain. The wisest, most mature character in the book (except the detective) may be a murderer. Agatha sometimes allows the killer suicide or a final heroic death to maintain a "good" character. So – it is the joy of Agatha Christie – the murderer may really be the last person you would suspect. And although the psychology may be shaky or the motive unconvincing, the clues will still be there in the incidents.

Go ahead. Search them out. And enjoy Agatha Christie as a wonderful puzzle partner. Some you'll win, some you'll lose.

SEARCH OUT THE CLUES AND ANSWER THE QUESTION – WAS IT N OR M?

THE

The Mind of Agatha Christie

After looking at her life and works, we start to have some picture of the mind of this well-bred, Anglo-American lady who called herself a low-brow, yet had tastes and interests that were upper-class without being aristocratic or huntin', shootin' and fishin'.

Notoriously, the worst aspect of this mind was its mild xenophobia and persistent anti-Semitism. While Agatha's admirers rightly insist that she never thought there was a "Jewish question" requiring radical political solution, and that she could occasionally portray sympathetic Jewish characters, they have been too quick to praise her insistence that she was shocked by her first encounter with ideological anti-Semitism. True, she was startled when Dr Jordan, German director of antiquities in Baghdad in 1933, said that Jews should be exterminated. But in general she was charmed by this doctrinaire Nazi. And it is naive if not disingenuous of Agatha's admirers to say that her references to Jews are trivial, and wonder why an unidentified reference in *The Hollow* led to protests from the Anti-Defamation League in 1947 and the demand from her American publishers that she forswear mentioning Jews and Catholics again. It almost surpasses belief that any patriotic Englishwoman, in the year when Belsen and Auschwitz had been exposed, should casually write about an ugly, brassy, overdressed and overpainted, grasping, greedy, bullying East End employer, with the overt message that a hard-working decent upper-class girl is tragically unlucky to serve this typical Jewess. When every possible allowance for her class and generation has been made, there can be no forgiveness for this crass insensitivity.

It is a pleasure to turn to the characteristics noted by Harvard scholar Gillian McGill. As a professor of women's studies, Ms McGill somewhat anachronistically dubs Agatha a feminist – hardly a fitting title for the apolitical renouncer of every -ism and regretter of liberated women's loss of gallant protection – Agatha never discusses suffragettes, but clearly felt the had sold their birthright of manipulative influence for the inferior pottage of political activism. Lady politicians and ideologues are invariably satirized in her works. But Ms Gill is absolutely right in noticing Agatha's pleasure in hard-working young women who make their own way in the world – even at the preposterous length of suggesting that a 22-year-old girl in *Crooked House* might have risen to a senior post in the Foreign Service. She is right, too, to note that Agatha, wife of a man 14 years younger than herself, often recognized and approved the fact that rich women might indulge themselves with younger lovers, and was generously uncensorious about the fact that rich old men are even more so inclined.

As a woman, Agatha always seems gloriously confident about her own femininity and sexuality and comments discreetly on men or spinsters to other sexually confident women. Lesbians and homosexuals give her no problems at all. Mr Pye in *The Moving Finger* is smiled at as "an old spinster": his sexual orientation would not be perceptible to the more innocent readers of 1942. Akhnaton's intense attraction to his military friend Horemheb in the unperformed play of 1937 does not confuse his emotional tie with physical desire – the stage direction calling Horemheb a "pukka sahib" reveals Agatha's dated outlook. Only in *Murder is Easy* (1939) does Agatha portray a really distasteful "pervert". Her red herring suspect Mr Edgeworthy seems to have been influenced by Daphne Du Maurier's *Rebecca*, since bisexual orgies prove to be his nasty little secret. Always a sounder moralist than Du Maurier, Agatha does not think this makes him deserve death.

Finally one should note that Mrs Christie always enjoyed a very slightly naughty, even schoolgirlish hidden joke. A classic example is the misnaming of Mrs Burke, "Mrs Burp" in *Mrs McGinty's Dead*. Such things were mildly daring in her gender and generation.

Travel

Ever since cheap charter flights began in the 1960s, we have become accustomed to the idea of visiting other countries. In Agatha Christie's formative years it was very different. Well-bred young ladies might complete their education at Continental finishing schools, as Agatha – and Ariadne Oliver – did in Paris and Miss Marple did in Florence. But those who went to the outposts of the Empire were a special and peculiar group. Those who patronized Thomas Cook's tours of the Alps, rarely thought of doing so as an annual holiday. Monaco and the French Riviera were available for the rich and raffish, but Agatha showed in *The Blue Train* that she was not impressed by them. Deauville and Dieppe offered licensed gambling for the upper classes and an escape from scandal for late Victorian aristocrats. Switzerland was also supposedly health-giving for tubercular Britons, and a short Swiss holiday was to be prescribable on the British National Health Service when it was first proposed.

POSTER FROM THE 1920S, DEPICTING TRAVEL IN THE FRENCH ALPS.

But Agatha's range of travel experience was really mind-boggling for her generation. France, Germany, Cairo. Even before she was married she had carried out what to many of her contemporaries would have made a lifetime's travelling. To the Pyrenees with Archie. Round the colonies and dominions on which the sun never set with Major Belcher. The unforgettable journey on the Orient Express, after which the Middle East became familiar territory. Honeymooning with Max in Venice, Yugoslavia and Greece. Holidays in Germany, Austria, Switzerland. Visiting India, Pakistan and Ceylon in 1960. At the end of her life, the long postponed trip to the West Indies.

And how did this broaden her mind? Not in the ways expected by Peace Corps volunteers or *au pairs* today. In non-English speaking countries, she was always part of a party of visiting English. She never actually lived with the indigenous people and came to know by experience just how and why other cultures worked. With cosmopolitan experience that enabled her to write better descriptions of the desert than of Whitechapel, she was nonetheless not merely Eurocentric but Anglocentric in outlook. She was too well-bred to laugh at other nationalities for being different – except that she felt licensed to parody stereotypical French traits in Poirot the Belgian, the brave little refugee and detective hero. She was sufficiently half-

American that the standard Brit-centered parody of the loud-mouthed, pushy Yank plays no greater part in her work than the loud-mouthed pushy English politician. She was sufficiently Eurocentric that travelling parties and archaeological expeditions might contain perfectly acceptable western European members, who would normally be quietly spoken and held in the background of the action. But no Continental can ever match the dignity and authority of Race and Battle; the pluck and sprightliness of Tuppence and Bundle; the solidly decent reliability of Hastings and Dr Haydock.

She was also sufficiently Eurocentric that "natives" of underdeveloped countries were distant from her. Not exotic. Not squalid. Servants, but servants one would never approach as closely as Poirot approaches his man George. (Or, by the way, "Georges". Poirot is not consistent in calling him "Georges"; the impersonal narrative is not consistent in calling him "George". From book to book he varies, and one suspects that Agatha intended he should be christened George but addressed by Poirot as "Georges", and she did not notice when intrusive copy-editing regularized the spelling in individual books).

Agatha is not harsh or contemptuous about native servants. Just distant. They might as well be furniture. Or pet animals with funny little foibles. If the diggers knock off promptly at the signal for meals, they are "Fidos". Seen in reality, romantic places like James Elroy Flecker's Ispahan and Samarkand turn out to be more mess than romance. True, both these examples from *Murder in Mesopotamia* come from the voices of characters. But the attitudes are not far from Agatha's own. Tolerant, agreeable, but in the end patronizing and confident of her and her culture's superiority. The attitude of mind without which empire would be unsustainable.

BAGHDAD AT ABOUT THE TIME AGATHA FIRST VISITED.

At one instant Agatha seemed willing to approve immersion in native culture, when Poirot uttered a perfect and appropriate, "*Bismillahi ar rahman ar rahim*". But in context this is just a facile exhibition of his knowledge offset against Nurse Leatharam's insularity. For Agatha was not insular. She was, as I said, cosmopolitan; but cosmopolitan in an Anglocentric way which today is probably only to be found among diplomats.

But she was never parochial. If she never adapted to contemporary foreign cultures as societies of equal humanity with her own, she managed precisely that mental leap with respect to the foreigners' ancestors. Foreign travel broadened Agatha's mind most remarkably in her knowledge of archaeology and preclassical history.

Archeology AND Ancient History

POT-BELLIED PHARAOH AKHNATON AND HIS BEAUTIFUL WIFE, NEFERTITI.

Agatha's interest in archaeology presumably took off from her intelligent churchgoer's knowledge of the Bible. Every educated person of her generation knew that the patriarch Abraham originally came from Ur of the Chaldees, and this had given Leonard Woolley's excavation its international fame.

But for all her practical work at digs over the next 30 years, the Sumerians never seem to have seized her interest. Her memoir of her pre-war archaeological years, *Come Tell Me How you Live*, was avowedly, "Not at all serious or archaeological", and like the notes and diaries she kept, paid more attention to landscape, people, food and simple creature comforts. Leonard Woolley's belief that he had found evidence of Noah's flood at Ur may not have deceived Max and Agatha. In any case, there was no obvious way in which a mythical man building an ark to save his three sons and all fauna from the wrath of God lent itself to an imagination that had trained itself into envisaging crimes in everyday life.

But Egyptology was becoming matter of great general interest. The sensational opening of Tutankamun's tomb had seized Europe's imagination. The popular press's lurid invention of a "curse of the mummy" to "explain" Lord Caernavon's untimely death, and the exploitation of Egyptian styles and motifs in art deco buildings, overcame the longstanding disappointment that the more Egyptian history was uncovered, the less it seemed to endorse the biblical account. Agatha toyed with the silly curse in the early story, "The Adventure of the Egyptian Tomb". One specific area of Egyptian history, however, was manifestly fascinating in its own right, the reign of Amenhotep IV, who changed the religion and art of hyper-conservative ancient Egyptian culture. Husband of the timeless beauty Nefertiti and founder of the liberated school of craftsmanship which brought such wonders to his successor Tutankamun, the "heretic Pharaoh" who renamed himself Akhnaton was and is a historical figure to fascinate the literate world.

Agatha wrote a very serious play about him. Oh yes, it

contained a murder to explain (in a way) the mild historical "mystery" of Akhnaton's failure, the almost instant destruction of his cult of the sun-god Aten and the reversion to the old conservative cult of Amun-Ra after the very short reign of Tutankamun. But while enjoying herself with a mixture of principled and malicious assassination of the sort that invariably occurs somewhere in dynastic autocracies, Agatha proved seriously interested in what she saw as the political realities behind the ancient power struggle.

And they were, she felt, much like the realities of 1937. Akhnaton's idealism, she decided, was motivated by a mysticism that rose above sterile priest-ridden orthodoxy. It was akin to that of the high-minded European pacifists who were in the ascendancy. As the fall of George Lansbury (dethroned from leading the Labour Party when he tried to take it on a pacifist crusade) had shown, such idealists might be lovable or admirable, but the common people would not follow them.

Yet, for the only time in her life, Agatha did not imagine a pacifist to be a treacherous "skunk" in league with a national enemy. True, she thought Akhnaton's policy was a predictable and inevitable failure. But her grounds were the realistic ones that most men are greedy, many are warlike and some are evil, and an alliance of the three will ultimately attack and over-run the modest and principled if they do not arm themselves. Agatha's Akhnaton is a true artist – fictitiously put forward as the sculptor of Nefertiti's head – though he is surrounded by decadent posturing charlatans. He is a true friend to the "*pukka sahib*" Horemheb, though the latter will be forced to succeed to the throne rather after the manner of a usurper for the public good. Nonmilitarism, uniquely in Agatha's work, is seen as being unhypocritical and honest, if misguided. The story of Akhnaton is a tragedy, written in the effective laconic style developed by Maurice Maeterlinck for timeless drama.

Yet the very modern feel of the characters (like those of Agatha's friend"Gordon Daviot's" *Richard of Bordeaux*) robs the play of any real sense of antiquity. Unlike Shaw in *St Joan*, Agatha had nothing new or perceptive to say about the past or her central issues. Nor was she blessed with anything like Shavian wit to persuade a producer to mount her hugely expensive costume drama. She remained proud of it, however, and saw to its publication in the 1970s.

MARY NEWCOMBE AS SHAW'S ST JOAN, REVIVING THE ROLE CREATED BY AGATHA'S FRIEND SYBIL THORNDIKE.

Her general view that historical personages were "just like you and me" gives an even more soap opera feel to her ancient Egyptian whodunnit *Death Comes as the End.* Characters who might have stepped out of *Mrs Dale's Diary* wear historical clothes and move around ancient dwelling places without ever giving us a real feeling of how different cultures make people's behaviour seem different. This was the book that led Edmund Wilson to describe her work as so mawkish and banal that it was "literally impossible to read". I shared the experience when I first tried to read it more than 30 years ago, and can still only acknowledge its success as a fair and soluble puzzle.

Music

Agatha Christie was a natural musician. Herr Schürmer's advice against her attempting to become a concert pianist rested on her temperamental inability to keep her nerve when performing in public, not any lack of talent. Yet her notorious shyness disappeared when she sang. The only thing stopping her from becoming a professional singer was the lightness of a voice unfitted for grand Wagnerian roles, and her contempt for the alternative of a concert soprano's career, singing *lieder*, ballads and arias torn from their full operatic context. As a writer Agatha was content to admit that she could not write like Graham Greene and Muriel Spark, and get on with earning her living by what she *could* write. As a musician, she refused to accept what she saw as second best.

The impression that she was by nature first and foremost a musician is supported by her continuing attitudes to music. Perhaps the strangest was her reported remark to a young friend in old age, "If I'd been an opera singer I might have been rich". Probably this extraordinary observation by an extremely prosperous woman is a tragic instance of the creative writer's typical anxiety about waning earning powers. It is certainly sad to see

AGATHA AT HER PIANO: MAX LISTENING.

Agatha's love of music reduced to a vulgar wish for the security of greater wealth. But it is also striking that her pinnacle of missed ambition in old age remained the goal of being a Wagnerian diva and singing Isolde. Those with "the right vocal cords," she declared in her *Autobiography*, were "the privileged few".

It is significant, too, that her first Mary Westmacott novel should focus sharply on questions of musical talent. *Giant's Bread* is so named after the beanstalk giant's threat to Jack the Giantkiller. Anti-hero Vernon Deyre's inescapable creativity will "grind his bones" to make the "bread" of music he hears in his head, regardless of the fact that his need to be a major composer is at odds with his other ambitions to marry his beautiful but unprincipled sweetheart, and to retain his old family home. The girl Vernon should have married, whose love for him and his music is uncontaminated by selfish materialism, is the operatic soprano Agatha herself would have loved to be. The music that introduces us to this novel's serious concern is Russian, and said to show the influences of Wagner, Schoenberg and Debussy. The public image of Agatha Christie would suggest that she might have admired English charmers like Rutland Boughton or George Butterworth or Percy Grainger. One would never have predicted a respect for Schoenberg, the late romantic whose music baffled the conventional by adopting the 12-tone scale.

While she could not sing, Agatha continued to play the piano. Its importance for her was marked by her need to return to Ashfield and Clara's piano from time to time when she and Archie lived in London flats and could not keep one of their own. In London, she was conscientiously aware that playing the piano could disturb the neighbours, and had to cease at a given hour. *In the Mirror Crack'd from Side to Side* she has a character voice her classical music-loving generation's belief that the neighbours should be in some way gratified that they played good and improving music.

In her detective fiction, Agatha eschewed Conan Doyle's trick of making the detective a passionate intellectual music-lover whose taste has nothing to do with his detective ability. Miss Marple once reflects that a little treat she might give herself with a lot of money would be occasional visits to the opera. Nothing elsewhere in her village life has suggested that music is important to her.

KARL CZERNY, COMPOSER OF CLASSIC EXERCISES FOR THE PIANO.

They Do It With Mirrors is a key text for assessing Agatha Christie the amateur pianist and music-lover as she chose to be seen by her public. Opening up the piano stool reveals the contrasting tastes of an old-fashioned industrialist and a modern young man. The industrialist has sheet music for Handel's *Largo*, Chopin *Preludes*, Mozart, and a Victorian ballad. The Largo (adapted from an operatic aria) and the ballad are surely signs that Agatha quietly knows her own taste to be better. And this music is accessible to players of relatively limited technical ability. Agatha, who probably played to concert standard, could no doubt have been much more ambitious.

The modern young man has music by Hindemith and Shostakovich. Agatha makes no comment on their music, but allows an aside on the outlandish names of the ultramodern to suggest a sympathy with their Philistine decriers that she may not really have felt. Neither man is said to have any Bach or Beethoven, perhaps too demanding for the industrialist and too conventional for the modernist.

But in the heart of the piano stool, and quite unpredictable, lies Czerny. The classic collection of dull and increasingly demanding five-finger exercises. Whatever her characters' musical taste, Agatha expected that they must practise and keep their technique up to scratch if they were to be taken seriously. In this above all, we must see her as innately a genuine and serious musician.

The Arts

A fine musician she might be. A graphic artist, Agatha was not. This had been firmly established when she was demoted to photographing rather than drawing archaeological finds from the Tells. But, as her photography had shown, she was not without a sense of composition and contrast. And she never hesitated to express views on art in her novels. They were not necessarily hers, indeed, they are most frequently used to exemplify her characters' personality traits.

In *They Do it With Mirrors*, for example, the elderly industrialist's visual taste is again contrasted with that of a young modern. The late Mr Gulbrandsen collected Thorvaldsen statuary. His posthumous stepson the theatre designer would shudder at such things. The reader is less likely than Agatha apparently imagined to be familiar with the inoffensive Danish neoclassical sculptor, much of whose work is held in a dedicated museum in Copenhagen. But it certainly matches Mr Gulbrandsen's taste for Chopin's *Preludes* and a piano arrangement of Handel's *Largo*. And since Gulbrandsen was Scandinavian, he was more likely than an English businessman to be aware of Thorvaldsen.

C.R.W. NEWINSON, THE "VORTICIST" PAINTER AGATHA ADMIRED.

Bad taste lies at the heart of *After the Funeral*. Cora Lansquenet's deceased artist husband was not only a bit of a bounder, he painted atrocious pictures. Bold nudes with heavy detail but dreadful draughtsmanship, they sound the sort of thing to be seen among the landscapes and still lifes at local art shows. Although she was no prude herself, Agatha presents most of the rare observation of dreadful Lansquenets through elderly and slightly old maidish eyes, and manages very discreetly to convey the idea that the late Pierre Lansquenet took a lascivious interest in his models which proved detrimental to his art. The use of an intelligent and up-to-date young woman to shudder at his painting of a buxom woman stepping into a bath, however, ensures that we should not imagine we are seeing a lot of silly old trouts behaving like E.M. Forster caricatures and deeming a nude "a pity".

Cora's own watercolours of real south-western English places (Polperro, Anstey's Cove) are said to be ghastly picture-postcard picturesques. And to make sure we understand fully that she is a woman of truly atrocious taste we are shown her preference for garish painted furniture over good antiques. This is all important in a plot which turns on her general inability to tell an old master from an old daub, provided each is dirty enough.

Miss Marple, of course, is being amiably characterized as a Victorian minded old dear when she prefers Leighton and Alma-Tadema to Joan West's paintings of "square people with curious bulges on them". Poirot's taste might be expected to be modern, given his passion for things square and symmetrical. But this appears not to be the case. In *Third Girl* he views the offerings of the

LORD LEIGHTON'S "FLAMING JUNE" THE SORT OF PAINTING MISS MARPLE APPROVED.

Wedderburn Gallery with distaste. Elongated cows against distorted windmills, all coloured purple. A lop-sided orange diamond with two human eyes suspended from it. This is "modern art" as excoriated by Disgusted of Budleigh Salterton. While admitting at once that charlatanical talents like those of Salvador Dali or Andy Warhol encourage talentless imitation, I cannot avoid the suspicion that Agatha is deliberately playing down to her audience here.

For her own tangential references indicate that she liked the work of C.R.W. Nevinson, especially *The Witch*. And Nevinson, while best known for his World War One paintings of Bapaume, was stylistically formed by Wyndham Lewis's Vorticist movement – a London school deriving from Cubism and Futurism. And if Agatha could enjoy Vorticism in the teeth of Lewis's rebarbative self-advertisement, she certainly did not share the retired Indian army officer's loathing of modern art or Miss Marple's reservations about square people with mysterious bulges. Not that liking Nevinson placed her securely among the intellectual *avant garde*. TS Eliot's cancelled early drafts of *The Waste Land* include a passage where the offensive "carbuncular" young clerk who casually seduces the typist equally casually remarks that Nevinson is the sort of chap worth getting to know if one wants to be accepted by the art crowd.

"A Portrait of the Artist as an Old Ram" is created in Agatha's best known painter character, Amyas Crale, the buccaneering victim in *Five Little Pigs*. The likeness to Augustus John has often been pointed out, and Agatha appears to support the view – certainly John's! – that painters who live only for their art may womanize and treat other people disgustingly, and all must be forgiven them. Since we now know that John might make passes at his own daughters when drunk enough, one must clear Agatha of approving quite such artistic licence. And also note that while Amyas has often been compared with Joyce Carey's Gulley Jimpson in *The Horse's Mouth*, he is less anarchic and has none of the similarities to Stanley Spencer which mark Carey's creation.

Literature

"THE LADY OF SHALLOTT" BY J.W. WATERHOUSE.

Like most writers, Agatha Christie was a voracious reader. A complete listing of the books referred to in her own works would give no idea of the huge range of writing she devoured. Thrillers, detective fiction, biography, essays and criticism, poetry. New novels by highbrows, lowbrows and middlebrows covering the span of her adult lifetime. Swapping opinions with Max in the 1940s about the greatest twentieth-century writers, she was definite about Shaw, wondered about Wells, Bennett and Galsworthy, wanted to let 20 years go by before deciding about Kipling. In the same period she asked Billy Collins to send her a range of recent books. As someone who rather disliked radio (and later television) she fed her mind from the printed page.

She shared her tastes with Max. Bridges's *Testament of Beauty* was poetry they both read while separated during the war, and Agatha was thrilled when he told her to look up a love poem in the *Oxford Book of Sixteenth Century Verse*, saying it was how he felt about her.

In her seventies she made a point of reading Fanon and Marcuse to see what was getting into young people's minds. And all her life she kept her familiarity with the classics fresh, re-reading the time-consuming Dickens and Shakespeare. Her romantic and positive treatment of mundane older men loving sprightly younger women in *Roger Ackroyd* and *Murder at the Vicarage* calls to mind the Jane Austen of *Sense and Sensibility*. Likewise *Why Didn't They Ask Evans?* includes a section when the attractive baddies seem to be enticing our hero and heroine apart, just as the Crawfords look likely to separate Edmund and Fanny in *Mansfield Park*.

Shakespeare gave Agatha the first quotation she used as a title – a fad of the 1930s, especially noticeable in Aldous Huxley. Her American publishers objected that *Sad Cypress* might be misread as *Sad Cyprus*, but in the end accepted the appropriately elegiac title for a book in which Agatha explored an emotion which had caused her so much suffering. Shakespeare also provided her with *Taken at the Flood* and *By the Pricking of My Thumbs*, as well as the Mary Westmacott title *Absent in the Spring*. It is fitting that the detective novel titles from *Twelfth Night*, *Julius Caesar* and *Macbeth* are all parts of quite familiar passages, immediately recognizable by the general reader. *From you have I been absent in the spring* by contrast is not one of the better-known sonnets. Like the Mary Westmacott title adapted from T.S. Eliot's *Little Gidding*

T.S. ELIOT (SECOND FROM RIGHT) CONTEMPLATING *MURDER IN THE CATHEDRAL*.

(*The Rose and the Yew-Tree*) it addresses a reader presumed capable of enjoying demanding poetry that will not necessarily turn up in the familiar anthologies.

Other poets she raided for titles were Blake, with the plangently apt *Endless Night*; Omar Khayyam for *The Moving Finger*; Flecker for *The Postern of Fate* and, twice, Tennyson for *The Mirror Crack'd from Side to Side* and *The Hollow*. The former is a familiar line from *The Lady of Shallott*. In quoting a little further from the poem, Agatha does something rather peculiar. Twice she bowdlerizes out the schoolchild's giggle over the line, "'The curse is come upon me', cried the Lady of Shallott", by changing "curse" to "doom". Then at the end of the novel she has one of the characters make the same prudish misquotation and comments on it. Maybe this was a sign that she was over 70 and starting to lose concentration. Or maybe she was teasing us. For in this novel, too, almost for the first time since the 1920s, she steps outside the anonymity of the authorial voice and addresses the reader directly with the amused remark on a prescription, "four grains of hy-ethy-dexyl-barbo-quinde-loritate or, let us be frank, some such name". Bearing in mind that Agatha was the only pharmaceutically-trained detective writer of her generation, the sly tease could hardly be bettered.

The Hollow represents something quite different. Here she exhibits the cultivated writer's bland assumption that the furniture of her mind is appropriate for any civilised person, and has Hercule Poirot quote the first four lines of Tennyson's *Maud*. Not the famous ballad section "Come into the garden, Maud", but the appropriately blood-boultered opening, "I hate the dreadful Hollow behind the little wood". Few of her readers can have known it, or known that the ballad is only a small part of a much longer (and pretty awful) Victorian epic of love, jealousy, a duel and a flight to the Crimean War.

Her non-fiction title *Come Tell Me How You Live* is taken from those great standbys of the literate English middle classes, *Alice in Wonderland* and *Through the Looking Glass*. The proverbial observer from Mars might well think that familiarity with Lewis Carroll's masterpieces was a compulsory prerequisite for writing books in twentieth-century England. Agatha quotes constantly from the Alice books throughout her career, rarely feeling any need to identify the quotations. The logic games of a playful academic mathematician were predictably much to the taste of a lady who had intuitively found figures more satisfying than grammar.

THE COOK, THE DUCHESS, THE PIG-BABY AND ALICE IN WONDERLAND.

Politics

"MILK AND WATER SOCIALISM": A CHRISTIE CHARACTER'S VIEW OF THE 1950S GOVERNMENT OF WINSTON CHURCHILL.

Party politics, Agatha declared, was anathema to her. Which makes it a pity she ever let political opinions stray into her books. Studying and defending a few party manifestos might have brought more sophistication and self-awareness to her. Canvassing and addressing envelopes might have given her a little sympathy with the sheer hard work the democratic process entails. And by mixing a little more with people who constantly thought about political questions, she might have come to distinguish between the cults of nationalism, efficiency, and youth and worked out a coherent stance toward the mass movements and -isms she casually thought of as a sort of literary *donné*: the unconsidered "enemy we always have to have" in thrillers.

THE ROMANTIC FACE OF FACIST YOUTH, WHOSE APPEAL AGATHA UNDERSTOOD.

It is in the thrillers that her political stance appears at its worst. Tommy and Tuppence start by opposing a *Secret Adversary* whose Napoleonic ambitions may be realized if he can engineer the "disaster" of a Labour government for Britain. Apologetically, a "good" Labour moderate who disapproves is mentioned. Could Agatha have imagined that some Labour leaders would meekly accept the role of permanently powerless pressure group the establishment preferred for them? As *Partners in Crime* the Beresfords are most frequently in pursuit of Bolshies, standard fare for a period when Agatha's friend Arnold Ridley wrote his great success *The Ghost Train*, with its staggeringly implausible alliance of Bolshies and Chicago gangsters gun-running on a remote Cornish branch line.

N or M reveals Agatha's poor understanding of her century. Something – probably Max's influence – compelled her to accept that any British Fifth Column would include some leading soldiers, politicians, lawyers and senior policemen. And she offers them the bland excuse that they would be understandably keen on the revitalizing efficiency of Fascism. Although, of course, Agatha insists that the decent bulk of the establishment always knew what a rotter Hitler was, it is not at all clear that she herself knew what was wrong with him, except that he dared to fight Britain. Thirty years later in *Passenger to Frankfurt*, she still feels that Fascistic German nationalism, attractively summoned by the horn motif from Wagner's *Siegfried*, might provide an irresistible basis for an international mass movement appealing to the most ambitious new young meritocrats. And they would collude with fomenting international anarchy to bring themselves to dictatorial power. Her bafflingly named part-hero Sir Stafford Nye may be intended to hint that the best Labour Party members of her own generation would have had nothing to do with it. It is a weird farrago to emerge from her self-educational reading of Fanon and Marcuse. But as in *N or M*, she takes it for granted that Fascists will want to recruit really able and decent people, like Tommy and Tuppence, and only their patriotism can overcome the allure of Fascist romanticism and efficiency. Always, she assumes that pacifist internationalism is inspired by would-be dictators. One can only guess that she was blinkered by her own relatively mild anti-Semitism, probably coupled with mild Francophobia and Germanophilia.

She is less offensive in the domestic politics of the detective novels. Poirot and other characters keep up a running grumble about high taxation and misplaced public spending on ineffective welfare measures throughout the 1940s and 1950s. A character in *After the Funeral* even calls the 1953 Churchill administration "mealy-mouthed milk-and-water socialists", no better than "that damned Labour government". But not only does this accurately represent a strong strand of middle-class thinking at the period, we have seen that Agatha personally had the best of reasons for finding the income tax unjust.

Her most ambitious Mary Westmacott novel, *The Rose and the Yew-Tree*, represents most perfectly her attempt to come to grips with the new politics of the post-war world. Starting from the 1945 election that swept Labour to power, she recognized that the old aristocracy's *noblesse oblige* Toryism could no longer attract the voters. She was not sympathetically aware of the misery laissez-faire economics had brought to the unemployed during the Depression. The industrial north of England, like the East End of London was foreign territory to her, and she always admired ruthless and buccaneering capitalists. So she wisely made no attempt to portray the real "new men" of the Attlee revolution, the Denis Healeys or Robert Maxwells who brought to Labour politics the sort of unbureaucratic adventurous drive she admired. Instead she imagined an unprincipled go-getting working man using his war hero status to acquire nomination as a Conservative candidate and battle his way up through a class system that, in the end, she could not imagine altering radically.

After all, she believed in a hero with identifiably working class legs! She really was sufficiently old-fashioned to feel a kind of species difference between men of different classes. Obviously politics could not remedy this. The true answers to human problems lay in religion.

EAST END BACK STREETS: A WORLD AGATHA NEVER KNEW.

Religion

CHURSTON PARISH CHURCH.

Few people knew that Agatha Christie was a serious and devout Anglican. Her overtly spiritual writing was fugitive and little-known: the short story "Star Over Bethlehem"; some poems; the last three Mary Westmacott novels. Hardly anybody connected them with the creator of self-styled "bon catholique" Hercule Poirot. The self-indulgent detective is no spiritual figure. He is never seen going to mass. He once appears with improper ecumenism singing "All things bright and beautiful" in an Anglican country church. He makes few moral judgements beyond the "bourgeois" disapproval of murder.

At a time when the highly unspiritual Enid Blyton brought out a children's *Life of Jesus*, few people would have regarded Agatha's rare and cautious ventures into religious writing as anything but formal, essentially commercial ventures. Again it was Dorothy Sayers, with her magnificent radio dramatisations of the gospels, who snatched public recognition as the devout Christian using her popular writing skills to propagate the faith.

Probably only Agatha's closest friends and family knew that she was perturbed by the threat divorce posed to her communicant church membership. When she decided to make the "thanksgiving" offering of a new east

ENID BLYTON, AUTHOR OF A CHILD'S LIFE OF JESUS, AMONG HER CHILDREN'S ADVENTURE STORIES AND FAIRY TALES.

window in Churston parish church, near Greenway, the diocesan authorities were not at first aware that charitable Mrs Mallowan was the famous Queen of Crime. The ladylike Agatha was almost silent about her beliefs. It was not good form to parade matters arousing deep and controversial feelings. And the Church of England was the haven of Ladies and Gentlemen. Well-bred people simply did not declaim, "I am an Anglican" like an evangelical declaring himself washed in the Blood of the Lamb or a Catholic apologist thundering about the True Church. Even C.S.Lewis, an atypical noisy convertite Anglican, carefully described his faith as "Mere Christianity".

But Agatha's faith was not just well-bred acknowledgement of proper forms and ceremonies. All her life she kept at her bedside her mother's copy of Thomas à Kempis's *Imitation of Christ*. And Clara – again without unladylike fuss or declamation – had been an almost eccentric religious personality. She alarmed her family by seriously contemplating conversion to Rome, and by flirtation with theosophy. She thought about joining the Society of Friends, and occasionally attended Quaker meetings as a spiritual battery charge even after settling into the "proper" religious resting place for a well-bred English lady as a moderately High Church member of the Church of England. Agatha dutifully followed her in this.

It is that copy of the *Imitation of Christ*, however, that is most illuminating in considering the faith of Agatha Christie. The first section, "Counsels on the Spiritual Life," outlines a profound and admirable basis which can be perceived underpinning Agatha Mallowan's life and Agatha Christie's writing. Here is the stress on accepting a background place in life; never wishing to shine in conversation; never pluming oneself on learning or status; even putting formal theology second to leading a life in Christ (as Agatha calmly dismissed the Annunciation as a doctrine she found unattractive, and drew on her own experience rather than church teaching to form her sexual ethics). Here, above all, is the insistence that the christian should not be forever judging others; not resting morality on a set of loudly proclaimed "thou shalt nots". Thomas à Kempis insists that all are tempted; all have fallen at one time or another; not even the great saints can guarantee their permanent state of grace. The Christian's mind must never be fixed on the sinfulness of other people. Here is the basis of that gentle tolerance which makes Agatha Christie whodunnits so much more acceptable than some of her more actively moralist competitors'. Here is the primary duty to lead one's own life with an unobtrusive decency outweighing all opinions, which makes Agatha's political and racial prejudices seem quite secondary.

And did Agatha find equal support in the later, more mystical parts of this great spiritual treatise? Probably. The evidence of the last three Mary Westmacott novels is that, like à Kempis, she profoundly believed that religious life began with a deep "conversion" from worldliness: believed, moreover, that such an offer of grace could be accepted or rejected, leading the potential convert to the unexpected sanctity of a Fr Clement (*The Rose and the Yew-Tree*) or the hell of self and self-justification (*Absent in the Spring*). Did Agatha's own sense of conversion come after the public humiliation of the missing eleven days, the hoax that failed and necessitated deceiving the public? Quite possibly. In *The Blue Train*, written during the turmoil of the aftermath, Poirot uncharacteristically tells the heroine that "*le bon Dieu*" drives the train of life. Agatha always found this book an embarrassment.

For she was always a lady. She respected privacy and did not impose her intense feelings on other people. And we do not know her deepest spiritual experiences.

C.S. LEWIS, ANGLICAN APOLOGIST.

Adaptations

"Beau Poirot' – about 40, maybe. Devilishly attractive to the ladies. Ensnared himself, though, by a pretty face when working out who on earth got into the locked study after the doctor left, and chatted with old Ackroyd before killing him. End the show with a touch of romance; old Beau Poirot in love heading for 'they lived happy ever after'. More satisfying for an audience than just that dreary round up of suspects, don't you think?"

Agatha didn't. She was justifiably horrified when this travesty of her creation was proposed. Michael Morton, a very experienced adaptor of novels for the stage, couldn't imagine a play without a love interest. Gerald Du Maurier, producer of the play *Alibi*, smoothed ruffled feathers on both sides, and came out with a compromise. Poirot should remain 60 and impervious to romance. But instead of the doctor's acidulous spinster sister observing all that went on, let there be a young and pretty *ingenue* lead.

Agatha accepted this, feeling that Morton had been decisively overruled. Perhaps making her think that was one of suave Du Maurier's greatest triumphs. He was the finest English actor of the day and his hyper-economical style, ultimately essential for close-up film work, had the sort of impact on acting that Garrick's replacement of barnstorming with realism had in the eighteenth century. For the compromise was, as Agatha knew, sacrificing the best character she had yet created. She believed that this irritation was probably the grit that formed the pearl in the oyster when she later resuscitated and modified Miss Sheppard as Miss Marple.

She took further revenge thirty years later in *Mrs McGinty's Dead* as Mrs Ariadne Oliver bewailed her collaborator Robin Upward's wish to make her elderly Finnish detective Sven Hjerson a 35-year-old romantic lead. And she reflected something of her own impression of working with theatrical people. Mother's boy Robin is given a slightly camp manner, as is the secondary character "Michael" the actor. The term "luvvies" had not yet been coined, but Agatha told Max that working with actors led her to start "calling all sorts of frightful people darling".

Of course, adaptation might necessitate changes. One of her mysteries is only solved by the discovery of a confession in a bottle, washed up at sea. This could hardly be staged satisfactorily. Agatha herself, thinking the play worth making, worked out the necessary changes to give a happy ending and an exposition of the plot.

She enjoyed working with stage people and visiting film sets. Her success justified lavish productions. The replica of the Old Bailey's no.1 court created for *Witness for the Prosecution* was one of the most expensive stage sets of its day. Agatha had to be restrained from hurrying over to Hollywood to see how filming the play was proceeding when Max went to the University of Pennsylvania to collect his gold medal. And her teasing remark, "Petronella will be there" in *Passenger to Frankfurt* followed her meeting the cast of *Murder on the Orient Express* and encountering Britain's best-known Trotskyist, actress Vanessa Redgrave.

Agatha Christie did not enjoy television. Its first postwar sallies in England were pretty dire. With Sir John Reith and his immediate acolytes convinced that radio was the educated person's medium, television limped along offering drama in studio sets that looked like large bare studio areas with a few flats and properties artistically placed. Boom shadow commonly fell over actors' faces, and the microphone boom itself occasionally swung into view above their heads. Agatha was relieved to have missed the televised version of *And Then There Were None* in which the general's dead body got up and strolled away with its hands in its pockets, blissfully unaware that it was still in vision.

Laughton, Larry and Rutherford

Part of Agatha's mild dissatisfaction with *Alibi* seems to have been dissatisfaction with Charles Laughton, the first stage Poirot. It is difficult to be certain, but she seems to have taken a mild personal dislike to Laughton. Unusually for her, she may have found his homosexuality distasteful. Her books certainly suggest that while she had no objection to minority sexual orientation in its own right, she detested the depravity – homo-, hetero- or bi-sexual – which flaunted itself in the promiscuous corruption of others. Laughton may have seemed to her awkwardly self-conscious.

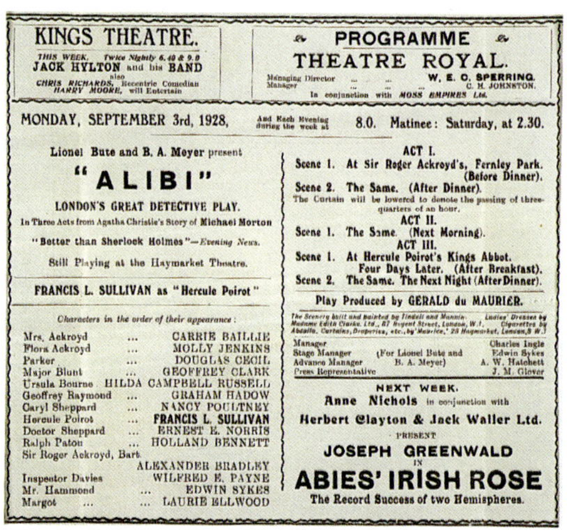
KINGS THEATRE.
THIS WEEK. Twice Nightly 6.40 & 9.0
JACK HYLTON and his BAND
also
CHRIS RICHARDS, Eccentric Comedian
HARRY MOORE, will Entertain

PROGRAMME
THEATRE ROYAL.
Managing Director ... ... W. E. O. SPERRING.
Manager ... ... C. H. JOHNSTON.
In conjunction with MOSS EMPIRES Ltd.

MONDAY, SEPTEMBER 3rd, 1928, And Each Evening during the week at 8.0. Matinee: Saturday, at 2.30.

Lionel Bute and B. A. Meyer present
"ALIBI"
LONDON'S GREAT DETECTIVE PLAY.
In Three Acts from Agatha Christie's Story of Michael Morton
"Better than Sherlock Holmes"—*Evening News.*
Still Playing at the Haymarket Theatre.

FRANCIS L. SULLIVAN as "Hercule Poirot"

Characters in the order of their appearance:

Mrs. Ackroyd ... CARRIE BAILLIE
Flora Ackroyd ... MOLLY JENKINS
Parker ... DOUGLAS CECIL
Major Blunt ... GEOFFREY CLARK
Ursula Bourne HILDA CAMPBELL RUSSELL
Geoffrey Raymond ... GRAHAM HADOW
Caryl Sheppard ... NANCY POULTNEY
Hercule Poirot ... FRANCIS L. SULLIVAN
Doctor Sheppard ... ERNEST E. NORRIS
Ralph Paton ... HOLLAND BENNETT
Sir Roger Ackroyd, Bart. ALEXANDER BRADLEY
Inspector Davies WILFRED E. PAYNE
Mr. Hammond ... EDWIN SYKES
Margot ... ... LAURIE ELLWOOD

ACT I.
Scene 1. At Sir Roger Ackroyd's, Fernley Park. (Before Dinner).
Scene 2. The Same. (After Dinner).
The Curtain will be lowered to denote the passing of three-quarters of an hour.
ACT II.
Scene 1. The Same. (Next Morning).
ACT III.
Scene 1. At Hercule Poirot's Kings Abbot. Four Days Later. (After Breakfast).
Scene 2. The Same. The Next Night (After Dinner).

Play Produced by GERALD du MAURIER.

The Scenery built and painted by Tindell and Mannin. Ladies' Dresses by Madame Edith Clarke, Ltd., 87 Regent Street, London, W.1. Cigarettes by Abdulla. Curtains, Draperies, etc., by 'Maurice,' 28 Haymarket, London, S.W.1

Manager (For Lionel Bute and B. A. Meyer) Charles Ingle
Stage Manager Edwin Sykes
Advance Manager A. W. Hatchett
Press Representative J. M. Glover

NEXT WEEK.
Anne Nichols in conjunction with
Herbert Clayton & Jack Waller Ltd.
PRESENT
JOSEPH GREENWALD
IN
ABIES' IRISH ROSE
The Record Success of two Hemispheres.

"LARRY" SULLIVAN APPEARS AS POIROT IN PORTSMOUTH.

It may also have seemed to her that Poirot's sexlessness needed some heterosexual bias. The ludicrous suggestion has been made – usually tongue in cheek – that Holmes and Watson might be seen as closet gays. The same charge could be levelled against Poirot with better supporting arguments. There is no apparent reason for his friendship with Hastings. There is something feminine about his punctilious neatness and cleanliness, his vanity, his feline observation of Hastings' attraction to auburn-haired girls. None of these things would have attracted curious glances in the early 1920s. But Agatha Christie, definitely a modern-minded young woman on sexual matters, might just have found sophisticated theatrical circles picking up a giggle she neither intended nor liked.

She herself commented on Laughton's bulk as making him inappropriate. But then, she approved the next stage Poirot, Francis L.Sullivan, who was even bigger. She may have disliked Laughton's make-up. Parting his hair in the middle didn't give his head a particularly egg-shaped appearance. His upper lip carried a slightly upturned toothbrush rather than a florid pair of waxed moustachios. And photographs of him in character suggests that he may have mugged excessively. Whatever the reason, Agatha Christie did not like Charles Laughton's Poirot.

Photographs suggest that Francis L.Sullivan's should have been even worse. He was huge and potentially a little sinister, (the Bumble of David Lean's *Oliver Twist,* and occasional mountainous, humourless Wehrmacht officers in war films). His false moustache was a pair of ludicrous spikes of crepe hair. But he probably maintained an air of dispassionate detachment that contrasted favourably with Laughton's feverish activity. And his immensity and fatness rested his head on puffy double chins and cheeks that might just have suggested the Poirotian egg-shape. Agatha liked him and his wife personally, dedicating *The Hollow* to them with a note apologising for having modelled the murder site on their swimming pool.

Her liking for Larry and Danae Sullivan may have led her to conceal still more disapproval of a misinterpreted Poirot. For when Sullivan expressed enthusiasm for a

MARGARET RUTHERFORD PLAYS HERSELF AS MISS MARPLE.

draft dramatization of *Death on the Nile* that she had prepared some years earlier, she insisted on cutting Poirot out and creating for Sullivan the new role of "Canon Pennefather". She was quietly amused by his thespian enthusiasm for the possibility of upping the Canon to a Bishop and costuming him in a purple silk front with a huge pectoral cross.

She also came to like Margaret Rutherford, though that lady's four Miss Marple films were an even worse travesty of Agatha's character. After a stage career which included successes in Ibsen and as the sinister housekeeper, Mrs Danvers, in *Rebecca*, Margaret Rutherford had settled for stardom as a character comedienne. She specialized in scatty but intrusive spinster roles: Miss Prism in *The Importance of Being Earnest;* the hopeless medium Mme Arkaty in *Blithe Spirit*, and Frank Baker's unjustly forgotten *Miss Hargreaves*, the incarnation of an organist's fantasy of a dotty old lady, who refuses to go back into his mind and get out of his physical life.

In 1960 MGM bought the film rights of a lot of Christie fiction, and commissioned their ancillary at Borehamwood to produce a low budget version of *4.50 from Paddington*. Quite reasonably, the producers simplified the plot to let Miss Marple witness the murder in an adjacent stationary train herself, instead of having a friend report it to her. And they let Miss Marple do her own sleuthing instead of employing Lucy Eylesbarrow. But they left little serious resemblance to the original novel and, barring her age, gender and spinsterhood, none at all to the character of Miss Marple. This was quite simply a vehicle for Margaret Rutherford to play her funny Margaret Rutherford role. She did it beautifully, and the film was a reasonable box office success in England, and played at art cinemas in America.

This prompted three sequels, which strayed further and further from Agatha Christie. The last, *Murder Ahoy*, made no pretence to have taken anything but Miss Marple's name from the books. Miss Marple is all gold braid, bo'sun's whistles and hornpipes as a senior Volunteer Reserve Wren. Like the earlier *Murder at the Gallop* it allowed Miss Rutherford to show that a woman could be even funnier than the transvestite males from Charley's Aunt to Old Mother Riley who have derived slapstick farce from old ladies being unoldladylike. Miss Marple fencing or doing the twist is a delight. But she is not, alas, Miss Marple.

Film Triumphs

Agatha quite liked the 1928 film. *Die Abentauer Gmbh* ("Adventures Ltd") a German silent version of *the Secret Adversary*. She didn't mind *The Passing of Mr Quinn*, made in England the same year. She hated Austin Trevor's three Poirot films, *Alibi, Black Coffee* and *Lord Edgware Dies*. The first really good Agatha Christie picture was *And then There Were None*, one of the excellent products of René Clair's mid-1940s spell in Hollywood. The cast was strong in older character actors Walter Huston, Barry Fitzgerald, C. Aubrey Smith and Judith Anderson. Clair exploited the period's wariness about violence to make the surprising post-mortem murderer's own death seem particularly realistic. The film stuck pretty well to the plot. The setting, like the original, was an empty building on an island. We can't blame Hollywood for eschewing the great art deco hotel on Burgh Island beloved of Edward VIII and Mrs Simpson (and Agatha Christie), in favour of a spookier, older building.

WITNESS FOR THE PROSECUTION: BILLY WILDER'S EXCELLENT SCREEN ADAPTATION OF AGATHA'S PLAY.

Progressively weaker remakes were produced in 1965 and 1975. The casts got younger and more glamorous, the action sexier and more violent. The settings changed to an Alpine mountaintop and the Iranian desert. The *New York Times* called the 1975 version a "Global disaster in Iran".

1957 saw Billy Wilder's magnificent version of *Witness for the Prosecution*. The original short story – a "how-can-we-get-him-off and what-really-happened?" suspenser – was notable for the double twist at the end. Converting this to a treble twist for the stage was a masterstroke, and stage and film versions continued *The Mousetrap*'s tradition of swearing everybody to secrecy about the solution. Marlene Dietrich played the pivotal role of the wife-witness, a part she had wanted ever since seeing it on the stage. Compelled by United Artists to insert a love-scene between Dietrich and Tyrone Power, Wilder sensibly collapsed it in comedy. And with Charles Laughton dominating the picture, well cast as the centrally observing barrister, Wilder again built up the comedy by giving him a heart condition tended by a bullying nurse, and a rather tedious running joke about wanting his Bermuda shorts packed for his holiday. But fidelity to Agatha's excellent plot and good acting by first-class players probably made this the most satisfying of all Hollywood's Christie films.

A tame version of *the Spider's Web* with Glynis Johns in the Margaret Lockwood role did not match up.

INGRID BERGMAN BOARDS THE ORIENT EXPRESS,

A version of *The ABC Murders* in 1966 was reduced to slapstick by a director who usually worked with Jerry Lewis. A version of *Endless Night* in 1972 was so badly edited as to be incomprehensible. And then in 1974 came the truly triumphant Agatha Christie movie. Sidney Lumet directed *Murder on the Orient Express* for EMI-Paramount, and an all-star cast of friends of Sidney Lumet rallied round to give the proceedings distinction. Lauren Bacall, Ingrid Bergman, Wendy Hiller, Vanessa Redgrave, Rachel Roberts, Jacqueline Bissett, Sean Connery, Anthony Perkins, John Gielgud, and Richard Widmark all supported Albert Finney as Poirot. While some of them gave brilliant cameos –notably Ingrid Bergman in an Oscar-winning role as a drab and inarticulate spinster missionary with poor command of English – and Finney's Poirot won the approval of Agatha Christie, it was the elaborate and period-perfect sets and costumes which set the tone for all good future filming of her work. Although two other costume dramas, *The Great Gatsby* and *The Lion in Winter* snatched the Oscars from *Murder on the Orient Express,* henceforth the best directors would realize that the appeal of Agatha made visible lay in "retro" nostalgia for the art deco period.

Finney's Poirot was the first to satisfy fans that they really were seeing a fussy little man with an egg-shaped head and extreme vanity about his moustaches, hair and appearance. It took a lot of padding to make Finney look small and give his head an egg shape. His moustache was satisfactory. But his hair was held down with an appalling blow-dried mixture of boot polish and Vaseline, making the fastidious Poirot look as though he had smeared his head with … boot polish and Vaseline!

CHARLES LAUGHTON IN *WITNESS FOR THE PROSECUTION.*

Murder on the Orient Express proved the most commercially successful British picture ever made. The lavish casting attracted huge audiences at the box office, as it had attracted celebrity and royal visitors to the studio (Vanessa Redgrave insisting on balancing the act with a visitor from the Socialist Workers' Party). Naturally EMI-Universal demanded a follow-up. *Death on the Nile* featured Bette Davis, David Niven, Angela Lansbury, Maggie Smith and Olivia Hussey. But Finney was not available to repeat his Poirot, and the role went to Peter Ustinov. Again an actor too bulky shambled his way through the role, and, as he recognized, was quite incapable of realizing Hercule's dapper vanity. Angela Lansbury went on to make a good Miss Marple in a version of *The Mirror Crack'd,* and thereafter featured in the Christie-inspired television series *Murder She Wrote.* Warner Brothers television also saw the value of Agatha for television, and made a couple of acceptable Miss Marples with Helen Hayes. They also resuscitated Ustinov's Poirot in two dull teleplays. But the first of these, *Thirteen at Dinner, (Lord Edgware Dies)* featured a chirpily sullen Inspector Japp created memorably by David Suchet.

Joan Hickson AND David Suchet

JOAN HICKSON'S MISS MARPLE SURVEYS *THE MURDER IN THE VICARAGE.*

Perfection came in the 1980s. In 1946 the 40-year-old Joan Hickson appeared in a minor role in the dramatization of *Death on the Nile.* Six years after Agatha Christie's death, the BBC decided to mount *The Body in the Library* and *The Moving Finger* as serials. Miss Hickson, by then 76, was suggested as an actress with much experience of straight roles in modern comedies and dramas who might make an excellent Miss Marple. She was not tall, like the image in Agatha Christie's mind. But her slim figure and serious gaze from deep-set eyes contrasted completely with the chubby, pop-eyed Margaret Rutherford's exuberance. And in 1982, the general public image of Miss Marple on the screen was Margaret Rutherford. Only dedicated Agatha Christie fans (like, of all people, the dissident Tupamaros terrorists in South America, who saw in Poirot and Miss Marple emblems of the struggle for social justice,) were likely to pay enough attention to the books to notice the vast disparity between comic Miss Rutherford and earnest Miss Marple.

Joan Hickson changed that overnight. She made the character quiet, reserved, confident and intelligent. She down-played the "fluffy old pussy" aspect, but never went the distance of being "the worst old cat in the village". She brought to the role a seasoned actress's skill at straightforwardly and unobtrusively becoming a given person with certain manners and mannerisms, without verging on caricature. Her quietly assured manner brought out the paradox of a ladylike spinster, well-bred without being aristocratic, coming to terms with violent crime, and never spilling over into absurdity.

The timeless English heritage quality of St Mary Mead was not overstated, either. The village and Miss Marple's cottage were picture-book pretty, but not exaggerated. The period was unobtrusively c.1955–1970. Miss Marple wore a shady straw hat such as any middle-aged lady might have worn for gardening at any period between 1930 and 1990 – just such a hat as Agatha wore at Nimrud. When I saw Margaret Rutherford filming *4.50 from Paddington*, her Agatha-style brown tweed suit and vivid green hat dominated the platform at Paddington Station. Joan Hickson would have sunk into the background anywhere. Only her steely, thoughtful gaze in close-ups marked her out from the crowd. She could be translated to Barbados for *A Caribbean Mystery* – the 1964 outcome of Max and Agatha's holiday in the West Indies – without seeming incongruous. With a series of 12 Miss Marple teleplays completed, the BBC and American PBS television hold a useful hoard of good general entertainment with a touch of nostalgia for reshowing as a treat on special occasions.

The perfect Poirot, by contrast was created with retro Agatha to the fore. LWT Television's series was characterized by brilliant titles: moving silhouettes of a steam train, an ocean liner and an airliner, all unmistakably of the 1930s; all stylized in streamlined art deco. The producers seemed to have scoured England for every last Bauhaus building to give Poirot the clean and symmetrical surroundings he loved.

And what a Poirot! Like Joan Hickson, David Suchet combined firmly defined characterization with cool understatement. Poirot's fastidious and cat-like qualities were brought to the fore. His intelligence was never cast in doubt by over-excitement or boasting. The man's vanity and conceit were delicately expressed in a little mincing strut. His complacent confidence in "the little grey cells" showed in a restrained smirk, rendered inoffensive by a gentle kindly crinkling under the eyes. The "egg-shaped head" was conveyed by Mr Suchet's baldness, without recourse to artificial double chins. The wardrobe produced an array of immaculately tailored, stylishly old-fashioned suits which perfectly conveyed the dapper dandy who, as Hastings said, would be more distressed by a speck of dust on his coat than a bullet wound. This was one of those rare occasions when an actor perfectly realizes a novelist's conception which has not quite worked as a character on the page.

DAVID SUCHET AS POIROT.

Suchet's Poirot was superbly backed by Hugh Fraser's manly, wooden and utterly convincing Captain Hastings, and Philip Jackson's vaguely shambling and bemused Inspector Japp – a character whom Agatha never seems to have fixed at one particular size or manner in her mind. Every frame captured perfectly the look and feel of the late 1920s or early 1930s.

PHILIP JACKSON AS INSPECTOR JAPP.

The effect was paradoxically marred by Agatha's plots. To make up the numbers for three consecutive series, many of the Poirot short stories were expanded into two hour dramas. And, candidly, they didn't really work. Neither the detection nor the suspense filled out into an evening's entertainment as the plots of the Miss Marple novels had for Joan Hickson. The series improved when the experienced television writers like Clive Exton, who made the adaptations, were given a freer hand to introduce their own fiction in teleplays based on the characters of Agatha Christie. But what characters! In the area where she had always seemed shallow, a medium which she despised finally revealed how narrowly Agatha missed making Hercule Poirot a veritable successor to the nonpareil Sherlock Holmes.

Index

Acknowledgements

The publishers would like to thank the following sources for their kind permission to reproduce the pictures in this book:

The Advertising Archives 104
All Saints Torre, Torquay 116
Copyright © BBC Photograph Library 3, 84, 118, 124
Bridgeman Art Library, London/Falmouth Art Gallery *The Lady of Shalott, c.1894 (oil on canvas) by John William Waterhouse (1849-1917)* 112/Museo de Arte, West Indies*Flaming June, c.1895 (oil on canvas) by Frederic Leighton (1830-96)* 111/Waterman Fine Art Ltd. *Cotswold Village by Adrian Paul Allinson (1890-1959)* 61tr
Corbis 29b/Bettmann 15, 28, 32, 41bl, 53tl, 57, 66tl, 72, 78/MGM/Selznick International 79bl, 86,117br/Hulton-Deutsch Collection 22, 27bl, 34, 49bl, 50, 64, 73, 75br, 87b, 91, 97tl, 99, 114tr, 117tl/Everett/EMI 20/Warner/First Artists/Sweetwall/ Casablanca 37/EMI/GW Films 76bl, 100, 123tr/ Historical Picture Archive 88/Edward O. Hoppé 60, 71/Archivo Loonografico 19/Monika Smith Cordaly Photo Library 42/Nik Wheeler 41tr
English Riviera Tourist Board 26, 59
ET Archive 80, 106
Mary Evans Picture Library 33tl, 70, 92/The Coupland Collection 62, 79tr, 87t/ Dorothy Wheeler 89b
John Frost 36
Hulton Getty 25, 38, 56, 81tl, 90, 97br, 107, 110, 113br, 115/Terence Fincher 95, 96/Radio Times 109/Topical Press 105
Ronald Grant Archive/Danzigers 2/EMI/Mersham/Titan 46, 67/63/Anglo Amalgamated/Harry Alan Towers 75t, 85br/Electric/Mass/Kinowelt/Haut et Court 98/120/MGM/Lawrence P. Bachmann 121/UA/Theme/Edward Small 122
Copyright © Rosalind Hicks 12-14, 16-18, 21, 23, 30/1, 35c, 39, 45br, 52, 53br, 54, 68, 85tl
Copyright © London Weekend Television Ltd./Granada Media 4, 29t, 66br, 69, 125
Raymond Mander & Joe Mitchenson Theatre Collection 1/Daily Sketch 35tr/51b, 77
Robert Opie 61br
Pictorial Press Ltd. 123bl
Popperfoto 6, 43, 44, 48, 55, 58, 83, 108
Topham Picturepoint 10, 24, 89t
Vin Mag Archive Ltd. 27tr, 40, 45t, 65, 74, 76br, 93, 101, 102, 114bl

Special thanks are due to Mrs. Rosalind Hicks, The Agatha Christie Society, Crime In Store, London, and Jean Reid at The Torquay Museum for their help.

Every effort has been made to acknowledge correctly and contact the source and/copyright holder of each picture, and Carlton Books Limited apologises for any unintentional errors or omissions which will be corrected in future editions of this book.